Latin
as an
Honour

Book 2

R C Bass

Latin as an Honour Book 2
First edition

ISBN: 978 0 9576725 3 6

Published by RCB Publications
Typeset by R C Bass

By the same author:
Latin as an Honour Book 1 ISBN 978 0 9576725 0 5
Latin as an Honour Book 3 ISBN 978 0 9576725 4 3
Latin as an Honour Answer Book ISBN 978 0 9576725 5 0
Streamlined Greek ISBN 978 0 9576725 8 1
Streamlined Greek Answer Book ISBN 978 0 9576725 9 8

Published by Galore Park:
Latin for Common Entrance13+ Exam Practice Questions Level 1 ISBN 978 1471 8534 5 6
Latin for Common Entrance13+ Exam Practice Questions Level 2 ISBN 978 1471 8534 7 0
Latin for Common Entrance13+ Exam Practice Questions Level 3 ISBN 978 1471 8534 3 4
Latin for Common Entrance13+ Exam Practice Answers Level 1 ISBN 978 1471 8534 6 3
Latin for Common Entrance13+ Exam Practice Answers Level 2 ISBN 978 1471 8534 8 7
Latin for Common Entrance13+ Exam Practice Answers Level 3 ISBN 978 1471 8535 0 0
Latin Vocabulary for Key Stage 3 ISBN 978 0 9036276 6 5
Latin Pocket Notes ISBN 978 1 9070477 1 8

Front cover: Arch of Septimius Severus, Leptis Magna (courtesy Wikimedia Commons)

robertcharlesbass@gmail.com
http://www.rcbass.co.uk

Celiae
uxori carissimae

… being so long in the lowest form I gained an immense advantage over the cleverer boys. They all went on to learn Latin and Greek and splendid things like that. But I was taught English. … And when in after years my schoolfellows who had won prizes and distinction for writing such beautiful Latin poetry and pithy Greek epigrams had to come down again to common English, to earn their living or make their way, I did not feel myself at any disadvantage. Naturally I am biased in favour of boys learning English. I would make them all learn English: and then I would let the clever ones learn Latin as an honour, and Greek as a treat. But the only thing I would whip them for is not knowing English. I would whip them hard for that.

Sir Winston Churchill
My Early Life: A Roving Commission (1930)

nil sine magno vita labore
dedit mortalibus

Life gives nothing to us mortals without hard work.

Quintus Horatius Flaccus
Satires 1.9.59 (35 BC)

Introduction

This book provides continuity and progression from Latin as an Honour Book 1, and is based on the ISEB Common Entrance Level 2 linguistic prescription. The rationale is the same: if you learn to write in Latin from the word go, it does not become a big deal later on, and it demands an inescapable thoroughness and attention to detail which can, to a degree, be side-stepped when working out of the language. The central aim is still for young learners to be able to read continuous Latin prose with a degree of fluency; it is just that the exercises which punctuate the reading passages (based on the Trojan War) are English–Latin rather than Latin–English.

Book 3, leading to Common Entrance Level 3, Common Academic Scholarship, and Public School Scholarship, is also available.

R C Bass
robertcharlesbass@gmail.com
www.rcbass.co.uk

Contents

§69 The Story of Troy (Part 1)

Exercise 69.1

*Discord, the goddess of arguments, gatecrashes
the wedding party of Peleus and the sea-nymph Thetis.*

1 olim in <u>monte Olympo</u> dei et deae <u>laetissimi</u>
   erant. cibum consumebant et vinum
   bibebant. <u>laetissimi</u> erant quod Peleus
   <u>Thetim</u> <u>in matrimonium ducebat</u>. Thetis dea
5 erant. Peleus vir <u>mortalis</u> erat. dei deae<u>que</u>
   laeti erant. ridebant. subito tamen
   Discordia, dea mala, intravit. <u>ceteri</u> dei, ubi
   Discordiam viderunt, non laeti erant. non
   iam ridebant. non ridebant quod Discordiam
10 non amabant. clamaverunt:

   'quid cupis, Discordia? cur hic stas? te non
   amamus. statim discede!'

   Discordia <u>nuntiavit</u>:

   'me audite, dei! me audite, deae! <u>donum</u>
15 habeo. <u>donum</u> pulchrum habeo. hic est.'

   deinde Discordia <u>pomum</u> <u>deposuit</u>. risit
   discessit<u>que</u>. dei deae<u>que</u> ad <u>pomum</u>
   <u>appropinquaverunt</u>. <u>pomum</u> spectaverunt.

Glossary:

monte Olympo = Mount Olympus
laetissimus, -a, -um = very happy
Thetim *is the accusative of* Thetis
in matrimonium duco (3) = I marry
mortalis = mortal
-que = and (*before the word it is attached to*)
ceteri = the rest of

nuntio (1) = I announce

donum, -i n. = gift, present

pomum, -i n. = apple
deposuit = (she) put down

appropinquo (1) = I approach

Exercise 69.2

1. From the passage on the previous page give, in Latin, one example of each of the following:
   (a) a verb in the imperfect tense;
   (b) a verb in the perfect tense;
   (c) a part of the verb *to be*;
   (d) an adverb;
   (e) an imperative.

2. **Discordia** (line 11). In which case is this noun?

3. **risit** (line 16). For this verb, give:
   (a) its person;
   (b) its number;
   (c) its tense;
   (d) the first person singular of its present tense.

Vocabulary 32	
and	-que
I announce	nuntio, -are, -avi (1)
I approach	appropinquo, -are, -avi (1)
the rest of	ceteri, -ae, -a (endings like the plural of *bonus*)

§70 -que (= *and*)

et is not the only way of saying **and** in Latin.

Another way is to use the word ending **-que**, but there is an important rule to note about word order:

-que <u>at the end of</u> a word is the same as an *et* <u>in front of</u> that word.

So:

Boys and girls   = pueri **et** puellae
                        = pueri puellae**que**

He is shouting and fighting. = clamat **et** pugnat.
                        = clamat pugnat**que**.

Exercise 70.1
1. Acca and Faustulus are happy.
2. Romulus and Remus are boys.
3. The farmers and the sailors are coming.
4. We are running and playing.
5. The friends are laughing and playing.
6. The slave is tired and happy.
7. The boy has food and water.
8. The boys are fighting against the farmers and sailors.
9. The farmers have spears and arrows.
10. The slaves enter and work.

Exercise 70.2
1. I am laughing and playing.
2. The boys and girls are running.
3. The slave is afraid and flees.
4. The men are running and playing.
5. The slaves and the masters are coming.

Exercise 70.3
1. The teacher warns the boys and girls.
2. The boys and girls do not fear the teacher.
3. The master enters and punishes the slave.
4. The girl enters and sees (her) friend.
5. The boys and girls are laughing and playing.

Exercise 70.4
1. Romulus and Remus were Romans.
2. We are laughing and playing.
3. The slaves are shouting and fighting.
4. The teacher punishes the girl and the boy.
5. The boys and girls listen to the teacher.

Exercise 70.5
1. The teacher was looking at the boy and girl.
2. The boy was afraid of the farmers and sailors.
3. The slaves had food and water.
4. The men were tired and miserable.
5. The temple was big and beautiful.

Exercise 70.6   TRIPLE STINKER
1. The slaves attacked (their) masters with spears and arrows.
2. The boys gave gifts and money to (their) good teacher.
3. The words of the bad and angry teacher were not good.

§71 The Story of Troy (Part 2)

Exercise 71.1

On Mount Olympus the three goddesses Juno, Athena and Venus argue over the golden apple.

1 dei deaeque in <u>monte</u> Olympo erant. <u>pomum</u> spectabant. <u>pomum</u> pulchrum erat. <u>pomum</u> <u>aureum</u> erat. <u>haec</u> verba in <u>pomo</u> erant: '<u>hoc pomum</u> <u>aureum</u> feminae 5 <u>pulcherrimae</u> est.'	mons, montis m. = mountain pomum, -i n. – apple aureus, -a, -um = golden haec = these hoc = this pulcherrimus, -a, -um = the most beautiful
Iuno regina deorum erat. <u>et</u> <u>soror</u> <u>et</u> <u>uxor</u> <u>Iovis</u> erat. dea Iuno <u>pomum</u> spectavit. verba legit.	et... et... = both... and... soror = sister uxor = wife Iuppiter, Iovis m. = Jupiter
'ego dea <u>pulcherrima</u> sum,' clamavit. 10 '<u>pomum</u> igitur meum est.'	
dea Athena <u>pomum</u> spectavit. verba legit.	
'erras, Iuno,' clamavit. '<u>pomum</u> meum est. <u>pomum</u> meum est quod ego <u>pulcherrima</u> sum.'	erro, -are, -avi (1) = I am wrong
15 dea Venus <u>pomum</u> spectavit. verba legit.	
'<u>erratis</u>, deae. ego <u>pulcherrima</u> sum. <u>pomum</u> igitur meum est. <u>pomum</u> <u>mihi</u> <u>tradite</u>!'	mihi tradite! = hand over to me!
sic tres deae de <u>pomo</u> <u>aureo</u> <u>disputabant</u>. 20 <u>omnes</u> <u>pomum</u> habere cupiebant. ad <u>Iovem</u> appropinquare igitur constituerunt. <u>Iuppiter</u> <u>et</u> <u>pater</u> <u>et</u> <u>rex</u> deorum erat.	disputo, -are, -avi (1) = I argue omnes = (they) all pater = father rex = king

Exercise 71.2

1. From the passage on the previous page give, in Latin, one example of each of the following:
   (a) an imperative;
   (b) an infinitive.

2. **pomo** (line 3).
   (a) In which case is this noun?
   (b) Why is this case used?

3. **deorum** (line 6).
   (a) Give the case of this noun.
   (b) Give the gender of this noun.

4. **erat** (line 6).
   For this verb, give:
   (a) its person;
   (b) its number;
   (c) its tense;
   (d) the first person singular of its present tense.

Vocabulary 33	
brother	frater, fratris m.
father	pater, patris m.
king	rex, regis m.
mother	mater, matris f.
mountain	mons, montis m.
parent	parens, parentis m./f.
sister	soror, sororis f.
wife	uxor, uxoris f.
both... and...	et... et...
I am wrong, I wander	erro, -are, -avi (1)
I hand over	trado, -ere, tradidi (3)

§72 Third declension nouns: masculine and feminine group

This is the largest noun group in Latin. There are two kinds of third declension nouns: masculine/feminine ones; and neuter ones.

In dictionaries and wordlists you will find four pieces of information about third declension nouns, set out like this example:

rex, regis, m. king
 1   2   3   4

1   The first word is the nominative and vocative singular.
2   The second word, ending in **–is**, is the genitive singular.
      If you remove this **–is** you will be left with the all-important **stem**. The importance of this will be seen shortly.
3   This letter indicates the gender: masculine, feminine or neuter.
4   This is the English meaning.

The way to work out the various endings of third declension masculine/feminine nouns is summarised in this table:

	singular	plural
nominative	(given in wordlist)	stem + **ES**
vocative	(same as above)	stem + **ES**
accusative	stem + **EM**	stem + **ES**
genitive	stem + **IS**	stem + **UM**
dative	stem + **I**	stem + **IBUS**
ablative	stem +**E**	stem + **IBUS**

By using the example of **rex, regis** (stem = **reg**-) and applying the above rules, we get:

	singular	plural
nominative	rex	reg**ES**
vocative	rex	reg**ES**
accusative	reg**EM**	reg**ES**
genitive	reg**IS**	reg**UM**
dative	reg**I**	reg**IBUS**
ablative	reg**E**	reg**IBUS**

Now practise chanting through the endings of the third declension nouns of Vocabulary 33 above.

Exercise 72.1

Give the:
1. accusative plural of *pater, patris m., father.*
2. genitive singular of *uxor, uxoris f., wife.*
3. dative plural of *mons, montis m., mountain.*
4. ablative singular of *mater, matris f., mother.*
5. genitive plural of *soror, sororis, f., sister.*
6. dative singular of *pater, patris m., father.*
7. ablative plural of *uxor, uxoris f., wife.*
8. accusative singular of *soror, sororis f., sister.*
9. accusative plural of *pater, patris m., father.*
10. vocative singular of *rex, regis m., king.*

Exercise 72.2

Give the:
1. genitive singular of *rex, regis m., king.*
2. nominative singular of *uxor, uxoris f., wife.*
3. dative singular of *mater, matris f., mother.*
4. vocative singular of *pater, patris m., father.*
5. dative plural of *frater, fratris m., brother.*
6. accusative singular of *mons, montis m., mountain.*
7. ablative singular of *soror, sororis f., sister.*
8. accusative plural of *mater, matris f., mother.*
9. ablative plural of *frater, fratris m., brother.*
10. genitive plural of *pater, patris m., father.*

Exercise 72.3

1. I have a brother.
2. I fear the mountain.
3. I do not have a parent.
4. I love my wife.
5. He fears his father.
6. He has a mother.
7. We have parents.
8. The mountains are high.
9. The king has a sister.
10. Kings have mothers.

Exercise 72.4

1. I warned my parents.
2. I used to have a sister.
3. We feared the king.
4. He killed the king.
5. We loved our mother.
6. We saw the mountains.
7. He loved his wife.
8. They saw the mountain.
9. She had a father.
10. The brothers and sisters were running.

Exercise 72.5

1. We saw many mountains.
2. We like the good king.
3. My parents were tired.
4. He has many sisters.
5. My wife is beautiful.

Exercise 72.6

1. The king had many wives.
2. The king's wives were beautiful
3. I have a beautiful wife.
4. The Roman kings were famous.
5. Mountains are high.

Exercise 72.7
1. The wife of the king is beautiful.
2. The king killed his own parents.
3. We often used to look at the high mountain.
4. The king had a brother and sister.
5. My mother had a beautiful sister.

Exercise 72.8
1. The boys were playing with their mothers.
2. The slaves fought against the king and his brother.
3. Tarquinius was the seventh Roman king.
4. Kings often give money to their wives.
5. The boy gave many presents to his good parents.

§73 The Story of Troy (Part 3)

Exercise 73.1

Jupiter passes the buck to Paris, prince of Troy.

1   tres deae, ubi ad <u>Iovem</u> venerunt, <u>haec</u>
    verba dixerunt:

    '<u>Iuppiter</u>, <u>pomum</u> <u>aureum</u> nos tres deae
    cupimus. quis est <u>pulcherrima</u>? lege! <u>nunc</u>
5   lege!'

    <u>Iuppiter</u> perterritus erat. iram dearum
    timebat.

    'deae,' respondit, 'vos <u>omnes</u> <u>pulcherrimae</u>
    estis. vos <u>omnes</u> <u>corpora</u> pulchra habetis.
10 ego legere non <u>possum</u>. est <u>iuvenis</u>, Paris
    <u>nomine</u>. in <u>urbe</u> Troia habitat. feminas
    pulchras amat. Paris <u>pulcherrimam</u> <u>leget</u>.
    Paridem rogate!'

    tres deae iratae erant. Paridem tamen
15 rogare constituerunt. itaque ad Paridem
    <u>ierunt</u>. <u>iter</u> <u>longum</u> non erat. mox igitur ad
    Paridem <u>advenerunt</u>. Paris, ubi <u>lucem</u>
    claram in caelo vidit, timebat. deae <u>omnia</u>
    de <u>pomo</u> <u>aureo</u> <u>narraverunt</u>.

20 '<u>Iuppiter</u> nos ad te misit, Paris. te deam
    <u>pulcherrimam</u> legere iubet. <u>nunc</u> lege!'

Iuppiter, Iovis m. = Jupiter
haec = these

pomum, -i n. = apple
aureus, -a, -um = golden
pulcherrimus, -a, -um = the most beautiful, very beautiful
nunc = now

omnes = all
corpora = bodies
possum = I am able, I can
iuvenis, iuvenis m. = young man
nomine = by name
urbs, urbis f. = city
leget = will choose

ierunt = they went
iter = journey
longus, -a, -um = long
advenio, -ire, -veni (4) = I arrive
lux, lucis f. = light
omnia = everything
narro, -are, narravi (1) = I tell

Exercise 73.2

1. From the passage on the previous page give, in Latin, one example of each of the following:
   (a) a preposition;
   (b) an imperative;
   (c) an infinitive;
   (d) an adjective.

2. **dixerunt** (line 2).
   For this verb, give:
   (a) its tense;
   (b) the first person singular of its present tense.

3. **deae** (line 8).
   In which case is this noun?

4. **habetis** (line 9).
   For this verb, give:
   (a) its person;
   (b) its number;
   (c) its tense.

Vocabulary 34	
city	urbs, urbis f.
light	lux, lucis f.
young man	iuvenis, iuvenis m.
body	corpus, corporis n.
name	nomen, nominis n.
journey	iter, itineris n.
river	flumen, fluminis n.
sea	mare, maris n.
task	opus, operis n.
I arrive	advenio, -ire, -veni (4)
I tell	narro, -are, -avi (1)
long	longus, -a, -um
now	nunc

§74 Third declension nouns: neuter group

These operate in the same way as masculine/feminine nouns like *rex, regis*, only different! You will see what I mean…

opus, operis n. task
  1   2   3 4

1   The first word is the nominative, vocative **and** accusative singular.
2   The second word, ending in **–is**, is the genitive singular.
        If you remove this **–is** you will be left with the all-important
        stem. The importance of this will be seen shortly.
3   This letter indicates the gender: neuter.
4   This is the English meaning.

The way to work out the various endings of third declension neuter nouns is summarised in this table:

	singular	plural
nominative	(given in wordlist)	stem + **A**
vocative	(same as above)	stem + **A**
accusative	(same as above)	stem + **A**
genitive	stem + **IS**	stem + **UM**
dative	stem + **I**	stem + **IBUS**
ablative	stem +**E**	stem + **IBUS**

By using the example of **opus, operis** (so the stem = **oper**-) and applying the above rules, we get:

	singular	plural
nominative	opus	oper**A**
vocative	opus	oper**A**
accusative	opus	oper**A**
genitive	oper**IS**	oper**UM**
dative	oper**I**	oper**IBUS**
ablative	oper**E**	oper**IBUS**

Now practise chanting through the endings of the third declension neuter nouns of Vocabulary 34 above.

Note the table of *mare, maris n. sea*, which differs slightly from that of *opus* (in the ablative singular, and the nominative, vocative, accusative and genitive plural):

	singular	**plural**
nominative	mare	marIA
vocative	mare	marIA
accusative	mare	marIA
genitive	marIS	does not exist!
dative	marI	marIBUS
ablative	marI	marIBUS

Exercise 74.1
Give the:
1. nominative plural of *nomen, nominis n., name.*
2. accusative singular of *iter, itineris n., journey.*
3. genitive singular of *corpus, corporis n., body.*
4. ablative plural of *flumen, fluminis n., river.*
5. dative plural of *mare, maris n., sea.*
6. dative singular of *iter, itineris n., journey.*
7. ablative singular of *nomen, nominis n., name.*
8. accusative plural of *corpus, corporis n., body.*
9. nominative singular of *mare, maris n., sea.*
10. vocative singular of *flumen, fluminis n., river.*

Exercise 74.2
1. You (pl) see the river.
2. We fear the sea.
3. The sea is deep.
4. My body is strong.
5. The journey was long.
6. I do not have a name.
7. I saw many bodies.
8. We do not often make journeys.
9. The name of the boy is Sextus.
10. I like rivers.

Exercise 74.3
1.   The mother was afraid of the river.
2.   The king was making a long journey.
3.   On the journey we saw many young men.
4.   The sea does not frighten sailors.
5.   The woman had a beautiful body.

Exercise 74.4
1.   The boy was standing in the river.
2.   The name of the young man was Marcus.
3.   We saw the rivers and the sea.
4.   The water of the river was deep.
5.   The waves of the sea were big.

Exercise 74.5
1.   My father often sails along across the sea.
2.   The slaves were carrying many bodies.
3.   There are many temples in the city.
4.   My friends were tired from the journey.
5.   I saw many bodies in the battle.

Exercise 74.6
1.   The king saw a bright light in the sky.
2.   I saw my mother and father in the city yesterday.
3.   The sailor's body was big.
4.   The young men were playing in the river.
5.   Sailors are not afraid of the sea.

§75 The Story of Troy (Part 4)

Exercise 75.1

The goddesses cheat.

1 Paris perterritus erat. respondit tamen:
 'omnes pulcherrimae estis, deae! nunc
 legere non possum. cras redite! cras
 constituam!'

> omnes = all
> pulcherrimus, -a, -um = very beautiful
> possum = I am able, I can
> cras = tomorrow
> redite! = return!
> constituam = I shall decide
> redibimus = we shall return

5 deae Paridi 'cras redibimus,' clamaverunt.
 iratae discesserunt.

 secreto tamen Iuno ad Paridem
 appropinquavit. haec verba Paridi dixit:

> secreto = in secret
> Iuno = Juno
> haec = these

 'si mihi pomum trades, ego te virum
10 potentissimum faciam.'
 postquam haec verba dixit, discessit.

> si = if
> pomum, -i n. = apple
> mihi = to me
> potentissimus, -a, -um = the most powerful
> faciam = I shall make
> postquam = after

 Athena quoque ad Paridem secreto
 appropinquavit. haec verba Paridi dixit:

 'si tu me leges, ego te virum
15 sapientissimum faciam.'
 postquam haec verba dixit, discessit.

> sapientissimus, -a, -um = the wisest

 postea Venus quoque ad Paridem secreto
 appropinquavit. haec verba Paridi dixit:

> postea = later

 'si tu me leges, ego tibi feminam
20 pulcherrimam coniugem dabo.'
 deinde discessit.

> tibi = to you
> coniugem = as your wife
> dabo = I shall give

 Paris solus nunc erat.

> solus, -a, -um = alone

Exercise 75.2

1. From the passage on the previous page give, in Latin, one example of each of the following:
   (a) an infinitive;
   (b) an imperative;
   (c) a personal pronoun;
   (d) a preposition.

2. **dixit** (line 11).
   For this verb, give:
   (a) its person;
   (b) its number;
   (c) its tense;
   (d) the first person singular of its present tense.

3. **Paridem** (line 12).
   (a) In which case is this noun?
   (b) Why is this case used?

Vocabulary 35	
after	postquam
alone	solus, -a, -um
husband, wife, spouse	coniunx, coniugis m./f.
later	postea
tomorrow	cras

§76 The future tense: 1st and 2nd conjugations

The future tense indicates an action which will take place in the future. The key English words here are *will* and *shall*. Here are the endings for *amo*-type and *moneo*-type verbs:

	1	**2**
	love	*warn*
I shall	ama**bo**	mone**bo**
You (singular) will	ama**bis**	mone**bis**
He/She/It will	ama**bit**	mone**bit**
We shall	ama**bimus**	mone**bimus**
You (plural) will	ama**bitis**	mone**bitis**
They will	ama**bunt**	mone**bunt**

Exercise 76.1
1. We shall stand.
2. They will carry.
3. I shall destroy.
4. He will have.
5. We shall approach.
6. You (sg) will hold.
7. I shall overcome.
8. They will fear.
9. We shall call.
10. She will fight.

Exercise 76.2
1. I shall answer.
2. You (sg) will see.
3. They will overcome.
4. She will laugh.
5. You (pl) will sail.
6. She will stay.
7. You (pl) will attack.
8. We shall stay.
9. You (sg) will kill.
10. I shall hold.

Exercise 76.3
1. We shall see.
2. They will watch.
3. They will have.
4. He will frighten.
5. You (pl) will hurry.
6. I shall move.
7. You (sg) will approach.
8. We shall hold.
9. You (pl) will enter.
10. They will ask.

§77 The future tense: the other conjugations, and *to be*

	3	3¹/₂	4	irregular
	rule	*take*	*hear*	*be*
I shall	reg**AM**	capi**AM**	audi**AM**	ero
You (singular) will	reg**ES**	capi**ES**	audi**ES**	eris
He/She/It will	reg**ET**	capi**ET**	audi**ET**	erit
We shall	reg**EMUS**	capi**EMUS**	audi**EMUS**	erimus
You (plural) will	reg**ETIS**	capi**ETIS**	audi**ETIS**	eritis
They will	reg**ENT**	capi**ENT**	audi**ENT**	erunt

Exercise 77.1
1. We shall rule.
2. I shall read.
3. You (pl) will arrive.
4. I shall run.
5. You (sg) will hand over.
6. We shall decide.
7. You (sg) will be.
8. I shall flee.
9. They will send.
10. You (pl) will desire.

Exercise 77.2
1. He will eat.
2. They will be.
3. We shall drink.
4. We shall run.
5. He will send.
6. We shall play.
7. You (sg) will read.
8. You (pl) will decide.
9. They will play.
10. I shall depart.

Exercise 77.3
1. She will flee.
2. You (pl) will be.
3. We shall write.
4. They will receive.
5. He will sleep.
6. We shall depart.
7. They will punish.
8. I shall be.
9. I shall throw.
10. You (sg) will put.

Exercise 77.4
1. We shall show.
2. You (sg) will sleep.
3. They will run.
4. We shall capture.
5. She will be.
6. I shall sleep.
7. I shall come.
8. You (pl) will take.
9. You (pl) will receive.
10. He will say.

Exercise 77.5
1. He runs.
2. He will run.
3. We rule.
4. We shall rule.
5. He will hurry.
6. He hurries.
7. She is.
8. She will be.
9. He will shout.
10. He will drink.

Exercise 77.6
1. He drinks.
2. They will show.
3. They show.
4. He will punish.
5. He punishes.
6. We see.
7. We shall see.
8. They will stay.
9. They stay.
10. They will be.

Exercise 77.7
1. You (pl) will carry.
2. They prepare.
3. I shall give.
4. We destroy.
5. We shall call.
6. You (sg) will destroy.
7. We shall sleep.
8. He will tell.
9. They have.
10. You (sg) read

Exercise 77.8
1. We sleep.
2. We enter.
3. You (pl) will laugh.
4. You (sg) will read.
5. I shall have.
6. They will arrive.
7. She will flee.
8. She flees.
9. They capture.
10. You (pl) will have.

Exercise 77.9
1. Yesterday I was looking at many beautiful girls.
2. Today I am looking at many beautiful girls.
3. Tomorrow I shall look at many beautiful girls.
4. Yesterday the Romans were carrying shields.
5. Tomorrow the Romans will not carry shields.

Exercise 77.10
1. Many young men will arrive tomorrow.
2. Help will come soon.
3. My father will be making a long journey.
4. The angry slaves will attack the walls.
5. The boys will hurry to the city.

Exercise 77.11
1. I shall drink wine tomorrow.
2. Boys will never listen to teachers.
3. The young man will hurry to the town.
4. The slavegirl will never prepare food again.
5. Good boys will always work.

Exercise 77.12
1. I shall come to the city tomorrow.
2. The king has a beautiful wife.
3. The woman has a good husband.
4. My wife was preparing good food.
5. We are making the journey now.

Exercise 77.13 TRIPLE STINKER
1. The water of the river is deep.
2. The wife of the king will not have money.
3. You (pl) saw the king on the journey.

§78 The Story of Troy (Part 5)

Exercise 78.1

Venus wins and promises Paris Helen, wife of Menelaus of Sparta.

1   postero die tres deae redierunt. ante
    Paridem steterunt. Paridi haec verba
    dixerunt:

    postero die = on the next day
    redierunt = (they) returned
    ante + acc. = before
    haec = these

    'Pari, deam pulcherrimam nunc legere
5   debes.'

    pulcherrimus = most beautiful
    debeo, -ere, debui + infin (2) = I
    must, have to, ought to

    Paris, quamquam iram dearum timebat,
    clamavit:

    quamquam = although

    'ego Venerem lego. Venus super omnes
    alias dea pulcherrima est.'

    super omnes alias = above all
    others

10 Venus, ubi verba Paridis audivit, risit. laeta
    erat. Iuno et Athena, ubi verba Paridis
    audiverunt, non riserunt. non laetae erant.
    iratae discesserunt.

    Paris Venerem spectavit. 'ego,' inquit, 'te
15 legi. mulierem pulcherrimam uxorem meam
    cupio. ubi est?'

    mulier, mulieris f. = woman
    uxorem meam = as my wife

    Venus Paridi respondit:

    'mulier pulcherrima Helena est. in Graecia
    in oppido Sparta cum viro Menelao habitat.
20 i ad Graeciam, cape Helenam, redi ad
    urbem Troiam! sic mulier pulcherrima tua
    erit.'

    i = go!
    redi! = return!

§78 The Story of Troy (Part 5)

Exercise 78.2

1. From the passage opposite give, in Latin, one example of each of the following:
    (a) a verb in the perfect tense;
    (b) a verb in the imperfect tense;
    (c) a preposition.

2. **risit** (line 10).
    For this verb, give:
    (a) its person;
    (b) its number;
    (c) the first person singular of its present tense.

3. **verba** (line 11).
    Give the gender of this noun.

4. **Paridi** (line 17).
    Give the case of this noun.

5. **Graeciam** (line 20).
    (a) In which case is this noun?
    (b) Why is this case used?

Vocabulary 36	
above	super + acc.
although	quamquam
before	ante + acc.
other	alius, alia, aliud
woman	mulier, mulieris f.
I go	eo, ire, ii/ivi
I go across, I cross	transeo, transire, transii
I go back, I return	redeo, redire, redii
I go in	ineo, inire, inii
I go out	exeo, exire, exii
I go towards	adeo, adire, adii
I perish	pereo, perire, perii

§79 Irregular verb: eo, ire, ii = *I go*

	Present	Imperfect	Perfect	Future
	go	*was/were going*	*went*	*will go*
I	eo	ibam	ii *or* ivi	ibo
You (singular)	is	ibas	iisti	ibis
He/She/It	it	ibat	iit	ibit
We	imus	ibamus	iimus	ibimus
You (plural)	itis	ibatis	iistis	ibitis
They	eunt	ibant	ierunt	ibunt
Infinitive ('to go')	ire			
Imperatives (go!)				
singular:	i			
plural:	ite			

Exercise 79.1
1. We are going.
2. They went.
3. They were perishing.
4. They are crossing.
5. We will return.
6. They went in.
7. I went out.
8. I will perish.
9. We were returning.
10. Go! (sg)

Exercise 79.2
1. I will go out.
2. I have returned.
3. They perished.
4. He has gone out.
5. You (pl) were going.
6. He crossed.
7. To go in.
8. They were returning.
9. We will go towards.
10. He returned.

Exercise 79.3
1. I will return.
2. They perished.
3. You (sg) were going.
4. They go in.
5. I went.
6. You (sg) will go.
7. I am going.
8. He is going out.
9. They were going.
10. They will go across.

Exercise 79.4
1. You (pl) go.
2. He returned.
3. I will go out.
4. They went.
5. They went towards.
6. I am perishing.
7. You (pl) will go.
8. We were going out.
9. He goes across.
10. I have returned.

Exercise 79.5
1. They will go out.
2. We were going.
3. He perished.
4. He will return.
5. She was going.
6. He is going towards.
7. We returned.
8. You (sg) are going.
9. I went out.
10. He went.

Exercise 79.6
1. They crossed.
2. He will go.
3. We go.
4. We will go across.
5. They are going.
6. You (sg) perish.
7. He was going out.
8. They returned.
9. They will go towards.
10. He will go out.

Exercise 79.7
1. They cross.
2. They will return.
3. We will return.
4. They perish.
5. You (pl) were going.
6. We perished.
7. We will go.
8. They go towards.
9. I was going.
10. We go out.

Exercise 79.8
1. I am already crossing the deep river.
2. We are going to the city.
3. Many men will perish tomorrow.
4. The beautiful woman is approaching the temple.
5. Many young men will go to the city tomorrow.

Exercise 79.9
1. Both mother and father perished in the war.
2. The young man was going towards the city.
3. I was going to the city with my friends.
4. We will cross the deep river tomorrow.
5. The women are going out of the temple.

§80 The Story of Troy (Part 6)

Exercise 80.1

Paris leaves Troy, goes to the Greek city of Sparta and kidnaps Menelaus's wife Helen.

1   Helena mulier pulchra et clara erat. in urbe
    Sparta cum viro, Menelao nomine,
    habitabat. Paris vir clarus erat. in urbe Troia
    habitabat. Troia erat urbs in Asia <u>sita</u>.

sita = situated

5   Paris ex urbe Troia ad urbem Spartam
    navigavit. ubi advenit, Paris e <u>nave</u>
    <u>descendit</u> et ad <u>regiam</u> festinavit. ibi
    puellam Helenam vidit. ubi Helenam vidit,
    <u>eam</u> statim amavit.

navis, -is f. = ship
descendit = disembarked, got off
regia, -ae f. = palace
eam = her

10 Paris Helenae 'te amo,' inquit, 'Helena.
    veni! ex urbe Sparta navigabimus et ad
    urbem Troiam ibimus! festina!'

    Paris Helenam ad <u>navem</u> duxit. deinde
    celeriter <u>fugerunt</u>. Paris et Helena ad urbem
15 Troiam navigaverunt. Paris laetus erat.
    Menelaus <u>autem</u>, vir Helenae, non laetus
    sed <u>iratissimus</u> erat.

fugio, -ere, fugi ($3^{1}/_{2}$) = I flee

autem = however
iratissimus = very angry

Exercise 80.2

1. From the passage on the previous page give, in Latin, one example of each of the following:
    (a) a conjunction;
    (b) an adverb.

2. **urbe** (line 1).
    For this verb, give:
    (a) In which case is this noun?
    (b) Why is this case used?

3. **nomine** (line 2).
    In which case is this noun?

4. **ibimus** (line 12). For this verb, give:
    (a) its person;
    (b) its number;
    (c) its tense:
    (d) the first person singular of its present tense.

5. **fugerunt** (line 14).
    Explain the connection between this word and the English word *fugitive*.

Vocabulary 37	
I flee	fugio, -ere, fugi (3$^1/_2$)
however	autem
ship	navis, navis f.

§81 The Story of Troy (Part 7)

Exercise 81.1

Menelaus appeals for help from other cities in Greece.

1   Menelaus iratus erat. iratus erat quod
     Paris uxorem, Helenam nomine, ad urbem
     Troiam duxerat. Menelaus hunc virum
     punire et hanc urbem delere cupiebat.

duxerat = had led
hunc / hanc = this

5   nuntios igitur ad omnes urbes Graeciae
     misit. hi nuntii haec verba dixerunt:

omnes = all
hi / haec = these

     'audite, omnes! Paris Helenam, uxorem
     caram Menelai, cepit. ad urbem Troiam
     fugit. propter hoc Menelaus iratus est.

omnes = everyone
carus, -a, -um = dear

propter + acc = on account of
hoc = this

10   hanc urbem delere cupit. arma parate!
     naves et milites colligite! ad urbem Troiam
     navigabimus et Troianos puniemus!'

arma, -orum n. pl. = arms, weapons
miles, militis m. = soldier
colligo, -ere, collegi (3) = I collect
Troianus, -a, -um = Trojan

     Graeci, ubi haec verba audiverunt, multas
     copias paraverunt. copiae Graecorum ad

copiae, -arum f. pl. = troops, forces

15   portum, Aulidem nomine, venerunt.
     Menelaus, ubi has naves et hos milites
     vidit, laetus erat. omnes salutavit. ad
     urbem Troiam statim navigare et bellum
     contra Troianos gerere et Helenam

portum = port
Aulidem = Aulis (a place name)
has / hos = these

saluto, -are, -avi (1) = I greet

gero, -ere, gessi (3) = I wage, carry on
libero, -are, -avi (1) = I set free

20   liberare cupivit.

Exercise 81.2

1. From the passage on the previous page give, in Latin, one example of each of the following:
   (a) an infinitive;
   (b) a preposition;
   (c) an imperative;
   (d) a verb in the future tense.

2. **nuntios** (line 5).
   (a) In which case is this noun?
   (b) Why is this case used?

   misit (line 6). For this verb, give:
3. (a) its person;
   (b) its number;
   (c) its tense:
   (d) the first person singular of its present tense.

Vocabulary 38	
arms, weapons	arma, armorum n. pl.
dear	carus, -a, -um
I collect	colligo, -ere, collegi (3)
I greet	saluto, -are, salutavi (1)
I set free	libero, -are, liberavi (1)
I wage war	bellum gero, -ere, gessi (3)
on account of, because of	propter + acc.
soldier	miles, militis m.
this (pl: these)	hic, haec, hoc (see table below)
troops, forces	copiae, copiarum f. pl.

hic, haec, hoc = '*this*' (plural: '*these*')
(refers to something near the speaker)

	masculine	feminine	neuter
SINGULAR			
nominative	hic	haec	hoc
accusative	hunc	hanc	hoc
genitive	huius	huius	huius
dative	huic	huic	huic
ablative	hoc	hac	hoc
PLURAL			
nominative	hi	hae	haec
accusative	hos	has	haec
genitive	horum	harum	horum
dative	his	his	his
ablative	his	his	his

(Grammarians call this a 'demonstrative adjective'. *monstro* means 'I show' or 'I point out'. In this case something near the speaker is being pointed out.)

Word order
hic haec hoc words usually come <u>before</u> the words they describe:

Examples   hic puer   *this boy*   (masculine singular)
                  hae puellae   *these girls*   (feminine plural)

Exercise 81.3
1. This soldier.
2. This king.
3. This shield.
4. This city.
5. These cities.
6. This slave.
7. This mother.
8. These boys.
9. These ships.
10. This gift.

Exercise 81.4
1. These bodies.
2. These kings.
3. These soldiers.
4. This journey.
5. This boy.
6. These slaves.
7. These farmers.
8. This river.
9. These words.
10. This wife.

Exercise 81.5
1. By this sword.
2. To this slave.
3. Of these women.
4. By this citizen.
5. By this name.
6. By these soldiers.
7. By these names.
8. For this young man.
9. By these rivers.
10. Of this king.

Exercise 81.6
1. For this girl.
2. Of these farmers.
3. To this queen.
4. By this road.
5. Of these Romans.
6. With these arrows.
7. With this food.
8. For this horse.
9. Of these walls.
10. Of this book.

Exercise 81.7
1. Of this girl.
2. Of this soldier.
3. Of these soldiers.
4. Of these ships.
5. By this gift.
6. By this war.
7. By this light.
8. Of this boy.
9. Of these slaves.
10. By these words.

Exercise 81.8
1. This boy is Marcus.
2. This war is bad.
3. These boys are small.
4. These girls are small.
5. I like this girl.

Exercise 81.9
1. I hear these words.
2. The king is punishing this soldier.
3. The girl does not like this food.
4. The master will give money to these slaves.
5. These rivers are long.

Exercise 81.10
1. The temple of this god is great.
2. The books of these boys are good.
3. I give much money to this boy.
4. I do not give money to these boys.
5. The master kills the boy with this sword.

Exercise 81.11
1. The master frightens the boys with these words.
2. I am reading the book of this boy.
3. When the young man heard these words, he departed.
4. The Romans will soon overcome the Greeks with these soldiers.
5. This river is sacred.

Exercise 81.12
1. The name of this girl is Flavia.
2. The walls of this city are tall.
3. The soldier has fought well with this sword.
4. The master will give a present to these slaves.
5. The girls liked the money of this young man.

§82 The Story of Troy (Part 8)

Exercise 82.1

The Greeks assemble at Aulis,
but their departure is delayed by contrary winds.

1 Graeci multos milites et multas naves
  Aulidem miserunt. Menelaus, ubi illos milites
  et illas naves conspexit, laetus erat. Troiam
  non amabat. illam urbem sine mora delere
5 cupiebat.

  naves tamen navigare non poterant. naves
  navigare non poterant quod venti adversi
  erant. Graeci prope naves diu manserunt.
  nihil faciebant. diu ventos secundos
10 exspectaverunt. nemo laetus erat. sed
  tandem venti secundi erant.

  Menelaus militibus clamavit:

  'comites, illi venti nunc secundi sunt. parate
  naves! parate arma! statim discedere
15 debemus!'

  Graeci, ubi haec verba audiverunt, naves
  celeriter paraverunt et Aulide navigaverunt.

Aulidem = to Aulis
illos = those
illas = those
conspicio, -ere, conspexi (3$\frac{1}{2}$) = I catch sight of
illam = that
sine + abl = without
mora, -ae f. = delay
poterant = (they) were able
adversus, -a, -um = contrary

secundus, -a, -um = favourable
exspecto, -are, -avi (1) = I wait for

comes, comitis m./f. = companion
illi = those

debeo, -ere, debui + infin (2) = I must, have to, ought to

Aulide = from Aulis

Exercise 82.2

1. From the passage opposite give, in Latin, one example of each of the following:
   (a) a conjunction;
   (b) a preposition;
   (c) a verb in the perfect tense;
   (d) a verb in the imperfect tense.

2. **manserunt** (line 8). For this verb give:
   (a) its person;
   (b) its number;
   (c) the first person singular of its present tense.

3. **naves** (line 14).
   (a) Give the case of this noun.
   (b) Why is this case used?

4. **verba** (line 16).
   Give the gender of this noun.

Vocabulary 39	
companion	comes, comitis m.
delay	mora, -ae f.
I catch sight of	conspicio, -ere, conspexi ($3\frac{1}{2}$)
I wait, I wait for	exspecto, -are, -avi (1)
no one	nemo
that	ille, illa, illud (*see below*)
without	sine + ablative

ille, illa, illud = '*that*' (plural: '*those*')

	masculine	feminine	neuter
SINGULAR			
nominative	illE	illA	illUD
accusative	illUM	illAM	illUD
genitive	illIUS	illIUS	illIUS
dative	illI	illI	illI
ablative	illO	illA	illO
PLURAL			
nominative	illI	illAE	illA
accusative	illOS	illAS	illA
genitive	illORUM	illARUM	illORUM
dative	illIS	illIS	illIS
ablative	illIS	illIS	illIS

(This is another demonstrative adjective – like *hic, haec, hoc*.)

Word order

ille illa illud words usually come <u>before</u> the words they describe:

Examples	ille puer	*that boy*	(masculine singular)
	illae puellae	*those girls*	(feminine plural)

Exercise 82.3
1. That sword.
2. That woman.
3. That war.
4. Those horses.
5. Those girls.
6. Those temples.
7. That delay.
8. Those companions.
9. That soldier.
10. Those soldiers.

Exercise 82.4
1. Those ships.
2. That light.
3. That name.
4. That city.
5. Those young men.
6. That journey.
7. Those rivers.
8. That danger.
9. That boy.
10. Those books.

Exercise 82.5
1. Of that boy.
2. Of that girl.
3. Of that war.
4. Of those boys.
5. Of those girls.
6. Of those wars.
7. For that slave.
8. To those slaves.
9. By those words.
10. By that present.

Exercise 82.6
1. To those companions.
2. For that soldier.
3. Of that ship.
4. By that light.
5. Of those bodies.
6. To those young men.
7. To that king.
8. To that city.
9. By that name.
10. For those friends.

Exercise 82.7
1. I like that girl.
2. I am watching those ships.
3. I am crossing that river.
4. I am setting free those slaves.
5. I am attacking that city.

Exercise 82.8
1. That slave is good.
2. That girl is beautiful.
3. Those soldiers are tired.
4. That ship is big.
5. That temple is big and beautiful.

Exercise 82.9
1. Those words are bad.
2. I do not like that boy.
3. The master often punishes those slaves.
4. The teacher does not like those girls.
5. The name of that boy is Marcus.

Exercise 82.10
1. The shields of those soldiers are big.
2. I shall give money to those slaves tomorrow.
3. The general gives weapons to that soldier.
4. The boy will kill the beautiful girl with that sword.
5. My mother will love those gifts.

Exercise 82.11
1. I like those words.
2. Many young men live in that city.
3. There are many ships on that river.
4. Where are the books of those boys?
5. That river is sacred.

Exercise 82.12
1. The teacher does not like those boys.
2. That ship will arrive soon.
3. The master never gives money to those slaves.
4. The master of those slaves is wicked.
5. The soldier wounded his friend with that sword.

Exercise 82.13
1. That master used to punish these slaves.
2. I saw this girl in that street.
3. Those slaves fled from this town.
4. This ship sailed towards that island.
5. Those young men were looking at these girls.

Exercise 82.14
1. Those soldiers attacked this city.
2. This master frightened that slave.
3. That slave was afraid of this master.
4. That girl likes this boy.
5. Many soldiers perished in that war.

§83 The Story of Troy (Part 9)

Exercise 83.1

Protesilaus: hero or idiot?

1   quod venti <u>secundi</u> erant, Graeci naves
    paraverunt. deinde in <u>eis</u> trans mare celeriter
    navigaverunt. ubi autem naves ad terram
    appropinquaverunt, nemo e Graecis e
5   navibus <u>descendere</u> cupiebat. <u>nam</u> dei haec
    verba Graecis <u>dixerant</u>:

    '<u>is</u> <u>qui</u> primus in terram <u>Troianam</u> descendet,
    <u>primus occidetur</u>.'

    diu Graeci nihil fecerunt. <u>inter</u> <u>eos</u> autem
10 erat miles, Protesilaus nomine. hic miles
    <u>mortem</u> non timebat. clamavit:

    'spectate me, comites! ego <u>fortis</u> sum. ego
    <u>audax</u> sum. ego primus in terram <u>Troianam</u>
    <u>descendam</u>. <u>sic</u> ego clarus ero.'

15 Protesilaus in terram statim <u>descendit</u>. ubi <u>is</u>
    descendit, ceteri Graeci <u>descenderunt</u>.
    postquam Protesilaus <u>Troianos</u> vidit, contra
    <u>eos</u> <u>ruit</u>. multos ex <u>eis</u> <u>occidit</u>. tandem
    tamen, postquam multa <u>vulnera</u> <u>accepit</u>,
20 periit. <u>sic</u> clarus <u>factus est</u>.

secundus, -a, -um = favourable

eis = them

descendo, -ere, descendi (3) = I climb down, disembark
nam = for
dixerant = had said

is = he
qui = who
Troianus, -a, -um = Trojan
primus occidetur = will be the first killed
inter + acc = among
eos = them
mors, mortis f. = death

fortis = brave
audax = daring

sic = in this way, thus

eos = them
ruo, -ere, rui (3) = I charge
occido, -ere, occidi (3) = I kill
vulnus, vulneris n. = wound
accipio, -ere, accepi (3$^{1}/_{2}$) = I receive
factus est = he became

Exercise 83.2

1. From the passage on the previous page give, in Latin, one example of each of the following:
   (a) a demonstrative adjective;
   (b) a third declension noun;
   (c) an ordinal number.

2. **venti** (line 1).
   Explain the connection between this word and the English word ***ventilation***.

3. **navibus** (line 5).
   (a) Give the case of this noun.
   (b) Why is this case used?

4. **fecerunt** (line 9). For this verb, give:
   (a) its tense;
   (b) the first person singular of its present tense.

5. **vidit** (line 17).
   (a) Give the Latin subject of this verb.
   (b) Give the Latin object of this verb.

Vocabulary 40	
among, between	inter + accusative
death	mors, mortis f.
for	nam
he, she, it	is, ea, id *(see below)*
I charge	ruo, ruere rui (3)
I kill	occido, -ere, occidi (3)
I receive	accipio, -ere, accepi (3$\frac{1}{2}$)
wound	vulnus, vulneris n.

Third Person Pronoun: *is, ea, id (= he, she, it)*

	masculine		feminine		neuter	
SINGULAR						
nominative	is	*he*	ea	*she*	id	*it*
accusative	eum	*him*	eam	*her*	id	*it*
genitive	eius	*his*	eius	*her*	eius	*of it*
dative	ei	*to him*	ei	*to her*	ei	*to it*
ablative	eo	*by him*	ea	*by her*	eo	*by it*
PLURAL						
nominative	ei	*they*	eae	*they*	ea	*they*
accusative	eos	*them*	eas	*them*	ea	*them*
genitive	eorum	*their*	earum	*their*	eorum	*their*
dative	eis	*to them*	eis	*to them*	eis	*to them*
ablative	eis	*by*	eis	*by*	eis	*by them*

Exercise 83.3

1. I have a son. I love him.
2. I have a daughter. I love her.
3. I have sons. I love them.
4. I have daughters. I love them.
5. I am looking at the temple. I like it.
6. I am looking at the temples. I like them.
7. I am reading a book. I like it.
8. I have a spear. I am carrying it.
9. I have swords. I am preparing them.
10. They listen to the words. They do not like them.

Exercise 83.4

1. His friends are famous.
2. Their slaves are good.
3. His weapons are new.
4. Her master is bad.
5. His slave is tired.

Exercise 83.5
1. I am preparing spears for him.
2. She is preparing food for them.
3. He is giving a gift to her.
4. I am giving money to him.
5. We are showing the island to them.

Exercise 83.6
1. The soldiers soon killed him.
2. The master punished them.
3. The king set him free.
4. Her name is Claudia.
5. We saw it.

Exercise 83.7
1. The kings punished them.
2. Father punished him.
3. The boys saw her.
4. The girl saw him.
5. I was waiting for her.

Exercise 83.8
1. The master gave the money to him.
2. The boy ran towards her.
3. I did not like his mother.
4. The king gave spears to them.
5. She saw him near the wall.

Exercise 83.9
1. His wounds are bad.
2. I was not listening to her.
3. She did not like him.
4. Their fields were big.
5. I have a book. Many words are in it.

§84 The Story of Troy (Part 10)

Exercise 84.1

The Greeks realise that capturing Troy will not be a five-minute job.

1 Protesilaus <u>mortuus</u> erat. Graeci contra
   muros Troiae ruerunt. fortiter et diu <u>sub</u>
   muris pugnaverunt, sed <u>frustra</u>. urbem non
   ceperunt. paucos Troianos <u>vulneraverunt</u>.
5 non multos Troianos occiderunt.

   Agamemnon, frater Menelai, <u>dux</u> Graecorum
   erat. non laetus erat. haec verba militibus
   dixit:

   'Graeci, haec verba <u>vobis</u> dico: Troiam hodie
10 non capiemus. muri Troiae alti et validi sunt.
   illi <u>cives</u> Troiani <u>fortes</u> sunt. muros bene
   <u>defendunt</u>. ego vos <u>castra</u> ponere iubeo.
   bene dormite! cras contra <u>hostes</u> iterum
   pugnare <u>debebimus</u>.'

15 milites Graeci verbis Agamemnonis
   <u>paruerunt</u>. <u>castra</u> posuerunt. fessi erant.
   mox dormiebant.

mortuus, -a, -um = dead

sub + abl = under
frustra = in vain

vulnero, -are, -avi (1) = I wound

dux, ducis m. = leader, general

vobis = to you

civis, civis m. = citizen
fortis, -is, -e = brave
defendo, -ere, defendi (3) = I defend
castra, -orum n. pl. = camp
hostes, hostium m. pl. = enemy
debeo, -ere, debui + infin (2) = I
must, have to, ought to

pareo, parere, parui + dat (2) = I
obey

Exercise 84.2

1. From the passage on the previous page give, in Latin, one example of each of the following:
   (a) an adverb;
   (b) a noun in the genitive case;
   (c) an infinitive.

2. **mortuus** (line 1).
   Explain the connection between this word and the English word ***mortuary***.

3. **muros** (line 2).
   (a) Give the case of this noun.
   (b) Why is this case used?

4. **ceperunt** (line 4).
   Give the first person singular of the present tense of this verb.

5. **debebimus** (line 14). For this verb, give:
   (a) its person;
   (b) its number;
   (c) its tense.

Vocabulary 41	
citizen	civis, civis m.
dead	mortuus, -a, -um
enemy	hostes, hostium m. pl.
in vain	frustra
leader, general	dux, ducis m.
under	sub + ablative
I defend	defendo, -ere, defendi (3)
I wound	vulnero, -are, vulneravi (1)

PRONOUNS

These are words which take the place of nouns, e.g. *I, You, He, We, They.*

First Person Pronoun: *ego.*

	singular		*plural*	
nominative	ego	*I*	nos	*we*
accusative	me	*me*	nos	*us*
genitive	mei	*of me/my*	nostrum	*of us/our*
dative	mihi	*to/for me*	nobis	*to/for us*
ablative	me	*(by) me*	nobis	*(by) us*
note:	mecum	*with me*	nobiscum	*with us*

Second Person Pronoun: *tu.*

	singular		*plural*	
nominative	tu	*you*	vos	*you*
accusative	te	*you*	vos	*you*
genitive	tui	*of you/your*	vestrum	*of you/your*
dative	tibi	*to/for you*	vobis	*to/for you*
ablative	te	*(by) you*	vobis	*(by) you*
note:	tecum	*with you*	vobiscum	*with you*

Nominative pronouns can add emphasis, or reinforce a contrast:

Examples:

You are bad; **I** am good.
*tu malus es; **ego** bonus sum.*

We are Greek; **you** are Roman.
***nos** Graeci sumus; **vos** Romani estis.*

I have been a good boy. (but others may not have been)
***ego** puer bonus fui.*

Exercise 84.3
1. You (sg) are playing; I am working.
2. We are Romans; you are Greeks.
3. We do not like you (pl).
4. You (pl) do not like us.
5. I do not love you (sg).

Exercise 84.4
1. You (sg) do not like me.
2. No-one saw me.
3. I love the girl.
4. The girl does not love me.
5. I saw you (sg) in the city.

Exercise 84.5
1. The enemy are attacking us.
2. The Romans do not like us.
3. My father likes you (sg).
4. I shall punish you, slave!
5. Who is calling me?

Exercise 84.6
1. The master is calling you (pl).
2. The woman is watching us.
3. Who will give money to me?
4. I will give money to you (sg).
5. The girls will play with us.

Exercise 84.7
1. The slave is standing near me.
2. The enemy are fighting against us.
3. My father is giving money to you (sg).
4. The master will give money to you, slaves.
5. The slaves are hurrying towards me.

Exercise 84.8
1. Friends are playing with me.
2. I will give a gift to you (sg).
3. The teacher never gives gifts to us.
4. My father gave a gift to me.
5. That teacher likes you (sg), not me.

Exercise 84.9
1. I am a Roman; you are a Greek.
2. We are good; you (pl) are bad.
3. I am giving money to you (sg).
4. He often gives money to us.
5. Play with me, friends!

Exercise 84.10
1. We do not wish to play with you (sg).
2. That girl will never give me a present.
3. The teacher will punish you (sg), but not me.
4. He is doing this for us.
5. Come with us, mother!

§85 The Story of Troy (Part 11)

Exercise 85.1

Hector, the son of King Priam of Troy, kills Achilles' friend Patroclus.

1 Graeci Troiam <u>oppugnaverant</u>. urbem Troiam tamen non statim <u>occupaverant</u>. Troianos non <u>vicerant</u>. prope urbem Troiam igitur <u>castra</u> <u>posuerant</u>.

oppugnaverant = had attacked
occupaverant = they had seized
vicerant = they had conquered
castra, -orum n. pl. = camp
posuerant = they had pitched

5 diu copiae Graecorum muros Troiae oppugnabant. eos tamen delere non <u>poterant</u>. <u>omnes</u> Graeci igitur <u>iratissimi</u>, Troiani <u>laetissimi</u> erant.

poterant = they were able
omnes = all
iratissimus, -a, -um = very angry
laetissimus, -a, -um = very happy

Priamus rex Troiae erat. multos <u>liberos</u>
10 habebat. <u>nemo</u> autem <u>fortior</u> <u>aut</u> <u>clarior</u> quam Hector erat. vir magnae <u>virtutis</u> erat. <u>pro</u> Troianis fortiter pugnabat.

liberi, -orum m. pl. = children
nemo = no one
fortior = braver
aut = or
clarior = more famous
quam = than
virtus, virtutis f. = courage
pro + abl = for
fortes = brave
fortissimus, -a ,-um = the bravest

inter Graecos quoque erant multi milites <u>fortes</u>. Achilles autem <u>fortissimus</u> erat. Achilles
15 amicum, Patroclum nomine, habebat. quod Hector Patroclum in proelio <u>occiderat</u>, Achilles <u>iratissimus</u> erat.

occiderat = had killed

Exercise 85.2

1. From the passage opposite give, in Latin, one example of each of the following:
    (a) an adverb;
    (b) a preposition;
    (c) an infinitive.

2. **oppugnaverant** (line 1).
    (a) Give the Latin subject of this verb.
    (b) Give the Latin object of this verb.

3. **erant** (line 8).
    Give the first person singular of the present tense of this verb.

4. **Troiae** (line 9).
    In which case is this noun?

5. **habebat** (line 10). For this verb, give:
    (a) its person;
    (b) its number;
    (c) its tense.

Vocabulary 42	
children	liberi, -orum m. pl.*see note below
courage	virtus, virtutis f.
for	pro + ablative
or	aut
I conquer, beat	vinco, -ere, vici (3)
I seize	occupo, -are, occupavi (1)

*Note: this word keeps its *e*. Do not confuse it with the plural of books, which doesn't! Compare the plurals of these words in the table below:

	books	children
nominative	libri	liberi
vocative	libri	liberi
accusative	libros	liberos
genitive	librorum	liberorum
dative	libris	liberis
ablative	libris	liberis

The Pluperfect Tense

This is the *'had'* tense. It is formed by taking the perfect stem (that is, removing the *-i* from the third principal part of the verb) and adding *-eram, -eras, -erat, -eramus, -eratis, -erant.*

	1	**2**
	loved	*warned*
I had	amav**ERAM**	monu**ERAM**
You (sing.) had	amav**ERAS**	monu**ERAS**
He/She/It had	amav**ERAT**	monu**ERAT**
We had	amav**ERAMUS**	monu**ERAMUS**
You (pl.) had	amav**ERATIS**	monu**ERATIS**
They had	amav**ERANT**	monu**ERANT**
	3	**4**
	ruled	*heard*
I had	rex**ERAM**	audiv**ERAM**
You (sing.) had	rex**ERAS**	audiv**ERAS**
He/She/It had	rex**ERAT**	audiv**ERAT**
We had	rex**ERAMUS**	audiv**ERAMUS**
You (pl.) had	rex**ERATIS**	audiv**ERATIS**
They had	rex**ERANT**	audiv**ERANT**
	3$\frac{1}{2}$	**sum**
	taken	*been*
I had	cep**ERAM**	fu**ERAM**
You (sing.) had	cep**ERAS**	fu**ERAS**
He/She/It had	cep**ERAT**	fu**ERAT**
We had	cep**ERAMUS**	fu**ERAMUS**
You (pl.) had	cep**ERATIS**	fu**ERATIS**
They had	cep**ERANT**	fu**ERANT**

Exercise 85.3

1. He had loved.
2. They had carried.
3. We had remained.
4. I had seen.
5. You (sg) had sent.
6. They had put.
7. We had made.
8. You (pl) had taken.
9. They had heard.
10. I had come.

Exercise 85.4

1. She had slept.
2. He had punished.
3. You (sg) had played.
4. He had given.
5. They had laughed.
6. We had fought.
7. They had departed.
8. I had read.
9. We had destroyed.
10. He had walked.

Exercise 85.5

1. They had made.
2. He had seen.
3. You (sg) had destroyed.
4. We had put.
5. I had laughed.
6. You (pl) had punished.
7. He had made.
8. She had sent.
9. We had come.
10. They had taken.

Exercise 85.6

1. We had loved.
2. They had taken.
3. You (sg) had heard.
4. He had ruled.
5. I had given.
6. He had led.
7. We had moved.
8. He had frightened.
9. They had answered.
10. I had sent.

Exercise 85.7

1. He had put.
2. They had run.
3. You (sg) had departed.
4. I had read.
5. We had slept.
6. We had walked.
7. He had fled.
8. You (pl) had made.
9. We had laughed.
10. You (pl) had destroyed.

Exercise 85.8

1. We had remained.
2. They had seen.
3. He had fought.
4. They had entered.
5. He had taken.
6. You (sg) had warned.
7. He had drunk.
8. He had said.
9. We had played.
10. You (pl) had killed.

Exercise 85.9

1. The teacher was angry because we had laughed.
2. The boy had not read the book.
3. The boys had been bad.
4. The girl had wounded the boy.
5. We had not heard the words.

Exercise 85.10
1. The master was happy because he had slept well.
2. The slaves had worked well.
3. The wife had departed.
4. The slave had prepared the food.
5. The friend had given much money to him.

Exercise 85.11
1. The enemy were happy because the Romans had departed.
2. The gods had conquered the Romans.
3. They had never destroyed the city.
4. We had arrived quickly.
5. They had taken many towns.

Exercise 85.12
1. The boy was running because he had seen the angry master.
2. The angry master had seen him.
3. The tired soldier had frightened her.
4. The young man had killed the general.
5. The wicked slave had wounded (his) sister.

Exercise 85.13
1. The boy had worked for a long time.
2. The leader had been angry.
3. The soldiers had fought well.
4. I had slept well.
5. The miserable boy had not laughed.

Exercise 85.14
1. The battle had been long.
2. The enemy had overcome many lands.
3. The master had set free many slaves.
4. The king of the enemy had hurried to the river.
5. The soldiers had attacked the city bravely.

Exercise 85.15
1. The slaves had run out of the town.
2. The teacher had read many books.
3. The messenger had said many words.
4. The slave had drunk much water.
5. The woman had received many wounds.

Exercise 85.16
1. The boy had sent a gift to (his) father.
2. The soldiers had gone across the river.
3. We had not caught sight of the girl.
4. The soldiers had not fought well.
5. The citizens had defended the city bravely.

§86 The Story of Troy (Part 12)

Exercise 86.1

Achilles, angry because of Patroclus' death, tells Hector that he will kill him. Hector is not impressed.

1   Achilles iratus erat quod Hector Patroclum
     occiderat. Hectorem igitur occidere cupiebat.

     olim Troiani contra Graecos prope urbem
     Troiam pugnabant. omnes fortiter pugnabant.
5   tum subito Achilles Hectorem in proelio forte
     conspexit. ubi eum vidit, ei clamavit:

     'audi me, Hector! ego sum Achilles, fortissimus
     Graecorum. tu vir crudelis es. quod tu
     Patroclum, amicum meum, occidisti, ego te
10 occidam!'

     Hector, ubi verba Achillis audivit, ei respondit:

     'audi verba mea, Achilles! laetus sum quod
     ego Patroclum, amicum tuum, occidi. ego te
     non timeo. tu me non terres. tu fortis non es. tu
15 audax non es. veni! pugna! victoria mihi facilis
     erit. ego te mox vincam!'

omnes = everyone
tum = then
forte = by chance

fortissimus, -a, -um = the bravest
crudelis, -is, -e = cruel

fortis, -is, -e = brave
audax = daring
victoria, -ae f. = victory
facilis = easy

Exercise 86.2

1. From the passage opposite give, in Latin, one example of each of the following:
   (a) a verb in the pluperfect tense;
   (b) an imperative;
   (c) a personal pronoun;
   (d) a verb in the future tense.

2. **urbem** (line 3).
   (a) In which case is this noun?
   (b) Why is this case used?

3. **conspexit** (line 6).
   (a) Give the tense of this verb.
   (b) Give the first person singular of the present tense of this verb.

4. **clamavit** (line 6).
   Explain the connection between this word and the English word *exclamation*.

5. **verba** (line 11).
   Give the gender of this noun.

Vocabulary 43	
all, every	omnis, -e
brave	fortis, -e
by chance	forte
cruel	crudelis, -e
difficult	difficilis, -e
easy	facilis, -e
everyone	omnes (m./f. plural of omnis)
everything	omnia (n. pl. of omnis)
noble	nobilis, -e
sad	tristis, -e
then	tum

Third Declension Adjectives in –*is*

e.g. fort**IS**, *brave, strong*

	masculine	feminine	neuter
SINGULAR			
nominative	fort**IS**	fort**IS**	fort**E**
vocative	fort**IS**	fort**IS**	fort**E**
accusative	fort**EM**	fort**EM**	fort**E**
genitive	fort**IS**	fort**IS**	fort**IS**
dative	fort**I**	fort**I**	fort**I**
ablative	fort**I**	fort**I**	fort**I**
PLURAL			
nominative	fort**ES**	fort**ES**	fort**IA**
vocative	fort**ES**	fort**ES**	fort**IA**
accusative	fort**ES**	fort**ES**	fort**IA**
genitive	fort**IUM**	fort**IUM**	fort**IUM**
dative	fort**IBUS**	fort**IBUS**	fort**IBUS**
ablative	fort**IBUS**	fort**IBUS**	fort**IBUS**

Exercise 86.3
1. A noble king.
2. Noble kings.
3. A difficult task.
4. Difficult tasks.
5. Brave soldiers.
6. All the shields.
7. All the girls.
8. Sad men.
9. A brave soldier.
10. Cruel wounds.

Exercise 86.4
1. A difficult son.
2. A difficult journey.
3. Cruel masters.
4. A sad girl.
5. A noble leader.
6. All rivers.
7. All the spears.
8. A brave leader.
9. Brave leaders.
10. Cruel women.

Exercise 86.5

1. The brave enemy.
2. An easy task.
3. A difficult book.
4. Noble men.
5. A difficult road.

6. Cruel words.
7. A cruel word.
8. Sad slaves.
9. A noble name.
10. A sad mother.

Exercise 86.6

1. By an easy road.
2. To the cruel boy.
3. For the brave soldiers.
4. Of all the girls.
5. By a cruel wound.

6. For the noble master.
7. With all the spears.
8. Of a brave boy.
9. For the noble girl.
10. By a sad book.

Exercise 86.7

1. I have a cruel master.
2. I am doing an easy task.
3. I love all wines.
4. I read all the books.
5. I am looking at all the girls.

Exercise 86.8

1. I am not carrying everything.
2. I am reading a difficult book.
3. I praise the brave leader.
4. I see a sad slave.
5. I am praising all the boys.

Exercise 86.9

1. I am setting free the brave slave.
2. I like all girls.
3. I do not like everyone.
4. I like difficult tasks.
5. I am killing the cruel master.

Exercise 86.10

1. I fear cruel soldiers.
2. I praise brave soldiers.
3. I am doing a difficult task.
4. I am carrying all the weapons.
5. I hear the cruel words.

Exercise 86.11
1. This soldier is brave and strong.
2. These soldiers are brave and strong.
3. That girl is noble.
4. This book is difficult.
5. My master is cruel.

Exercise 86.12
1. All the boys are working.
2. Why are you sad, boy?
3. I am sad because the master is cruel.
4. Not all tasks are difficult.
5. This king is noble.

Exercise 86.13
1. The cruel master punishes all the boys.
2. We are reading an easy book.
3. I do not like this difficult task.
4. All the girls are playing.
5. Not all teachers are cruel.

Exercise 86.14
1. The sad slaves fear the cruel master.
2. The noble master praises the slaves.
3. My brother is preparing everything.
4. We often make difficult journeys.
5. The slaves are sad because the master is often cruel.

Exercise 86.15
1. The noble queen was sad.
2. All boys like wine.
3. The cruel king punished the brave soldier.
4. All wars are cruel.
5. The journey was not easy but difficult.

Exercise 86.16
1. The soldiers had fought well.
2. We shall beat all the enemy.
3. All the citizens were afraid.
4. We do not like the cruel master.
5. That king is noble.

Exercise 86.17
1. The wounds of all the citizens are bad.
2. All the pupils have worked well.
3. It is not easy to work well.
4. The brave citizen fought against the enemy.
5. We came to the city by an easy journey.

§87 The Story of Troy (Part 13)

Exercise 87.1

Achilles fights Hector.

1 Achilles Hectorem spectabat. Hector Achillem
spectabat. Hector vir fortis et <u>audax</u> erat.
Achilles tamen <u>fortior</u> et <u>audacior</u> <u>quam</u> Hector
erat.

> audax = bold, daring
> fortior = braver
> audacior = more daring
> quam = than

5 subito Hector <u>telum</u> suum iecit. <u>telum</u> ad
Achillem <u>volavit</u>. in scuto tamen Achillis <u>haesit</u>.
Achilles, ubi hoc vidit, risit. deinde Hectori haec
verba crudelia dixit: 'tu me non occidisti,
Hector. ego sum <u>fortior</u> <u>quam</u> tu. ego sum
10 <u>fortissimus</u> omnium Graecorum. nunc ego te
occidam.'

> telum, -i n. = spear
> volo, -are, -avi (1) = I fly
> haereo, -ere, haesi (2) = I stick

> fortissimus, -a, -um = the bravest

ubi haec dixit, <u>telum</u> ad Hectorem iecit. <u>telum</u>
in corpore Hectoris <u>haesit</u>. Hector ad terram
<u>cecidit</u> mortuus. Achilles <u>laetissimus</u> erat. risit.

> cado, -ere, cecidi (3) = I fall
> laetissimus, -a, -um = very happy

Exercise 87.2

1. From the passage above give, in Latin, one example of each of the
   following:
   (a) a personal pronoun;
   (b) an adjective.

2. **spectabat** (line 1).
   (a) Give the Latin subject of this verb.
   (b) Give the Latin object of this verb.

3. **iecit** (line 5)
   (a) Give the tense of this verb.
   (b) Give the first person singular of the present tense of this verb.

4. **Hectorem** (line 12)
   (a) In which case is this noun?
   (b) Why is this case used?

Vocabulary 44	
bold, daring	audax, audacis
huge	ingens, ingentis
lucky, fortunate	felix, felicis
than	quam
spear, javelin	telum, -i n.
wise	sapiens, sapientis

Third Declension Adjectives in –*x*

e.g. feli**X**, *fortunate*

	masculine	feminine	neuter
SINGULAR			
nominative	felix	felix	felix
vocative	felix	felix	felix
accusative	felic**EM**	felic**EM**	felix
genitive	felic**IS**	felic**IS**	felic**IS**
dative	felic**I**	felic**I**	felic**I**
ablative	felic**I**	felic**I**	felic**I**
PLURAL			
nominative	felic**ES**	felic**ES**	felic**IA**
vocative	felic**ES**	felic**ES**	felic**IA**
accusative	felic**ES**	felic**ES**	felic**IA**
genitive	felic**IUM**	felic**IUM**	felic**IUM**
dative	felic**IBUS**	felic**IBUS**	felic**IBUS**
ablative	felic**IBUS**	felic**IBUS**	felic**IBUS**

Third Declension Adjectives in –ns

e.g. inge**ns**, *huge*

	masculine	feminine	neuter
SINGULAR			
nominative	ingens	ingens	ingens
vocative	ingens	ingens	ingens
accusative	ingent**EM**	ingent**EM**	ingens
genitive	ingent**IS**	ingent**IS**	ingent**IS**
dative	ingent**I**	ingent**I**	ingent**I**
ablative	ingent**I**	ingent**I**	ingent**I**
PLURAL			
nominative	ingent**ES**	ingent**ES**	ingent**IA**
vocative	ingent**ES**	ingent**ES**	ingent**IA**
accusative	ingent**ES**	ingent**ES**	ingent**IA**
genitive	ingent**IUM**	ingent**IUM**	ingent**IUM**
dative	ingent**IBUS**	ingent**IBUS**	ingent**IBUS**
ablative	ingent**IBUS**	ingent**IBUS**	ingent**IBUS**

Exercise 87.3
1. A brave soldier.
2. A cruel master.
3. A huge temple.
4. Lucky boys.
5. Wise teachers.
6. Wise words.
7. A daring leader.
8. A sad war.
9. Difficult battles.
10. A fortunate slave.

Exercise 87.4
1. A huge task.
2. Difficult masters.
3. Cruel brothers.
4. Daring enemy.
5. All the soldiers.
6. All the words.
7. A wise word.
8. Huge temples.
9. Brave slaves.
10. A bold king.

Exercise 87.5
1. The cruel master punishes all the slaves.
2. All soldiers are brave.
3. Not all wars are wise.
4. I never read difficult books.
5. We are building a huge temple.

Exercise 87.6

1. Rome was a huge city.
2. A wise leader always praises brave soldiers.
3. Not all kings are cruel.
4. We are doing a long and difficult journey.
5. The teacher praises the wise boy.

Exercise 87.7

1. All Roman soldiers were daring.
2. The sister of the boy is lucky.
3. All teachers are wise.
4. That girl has a wise brother.
5. Soldiers always like a lucky leader.

Exercise 87.8

1. The slaves are doing a difficult task.
2. All the slaves are working well.
3. We like the wise father of that girl.
4. We came to the city by an easy journey.
5. We will soon capture all the soldiers.

Exercise 87.9

1. That brave soldier is daring.
2. I have a wise father.
3. Soldiers like lucky leaders.
4. Not all men are wise.
5. The enemy were brave.

§88 Comparison

Comparison is all about comparing things. There are three degrees of comparison. These are called *positive*, *comparative* and *superlative*.
All the adjectives we have met so far are **positive** adjectives; for example: *bonus* (good), *pulcher* (beautiful), *fortis* (brave), *ingens* (huge).

Comparative adjectives in English usually end in *–er* or start with *more*
e.g.: tall<u>er</u>, small<u>er</u>, <u>more</u> beautiful, <u>more</u> interesting

Superlative adjectives in English usually end in *–est* or start with *very* or *most*
e.g.: tall<u>est</u>, small<u>est</u>, <u>very</u> beautiful, <u>most</u> beautiful

Here are some regular English examples:

Positive	Comparative	Superlative
tall	taller	tallest / very tall / most tall
interesting	more interesting	very interesting / most interesting
brave	braver	bravest / very brave / most brave

There are also some <u>irregular</u> examples in English:

Positive	Comparative	Superlative
good	better (not *gooder!*)	best (not *goodest!*) / very good
bad	worse (not *badder!*)	worst (not *baddest!*) / very bad
many	more (not *manyer!*)	most (not *manyest!*) / very many

How comparison works in Latin is shown in the table on the next page.

Comparison in Latin

Here are some examples:

	Positive	Comparative	Superlative
-us		**STEM + IOR**	**STEM + ISSIMUS**
	altus	altior	altissimus
	high	*higher*	*highest/very high*
-er		**STEM + IOR**	**POSITIVE + RIMUS**
	miser	miserior	miserrimus
	miserable	*more miserable*	*very miserable*
	pulcher	pulchrior	pulcherrimus
	beautiful	*more beautiful*	*very beautiful*
-is		**STEM + IOR**	**STEM + ISSIMUS**
	fortis	fortior	fortissimus
	brave	*more brave*	*very brave, the bravest*
-x	felix, felicis	felicior	felicissimus
	fortunate	*more fortunate*	*very fortunate*
-ns	ingens, ingentis	ingentior	ingentissimus
	huge	*more huge*	*very huge*
note:	facilis	facilior	facillimus
	easy	*easier*	*very easy, the easiest*
	difficilis	difficilior	difficillimus
	difficult	*more difficult*	*very difficult, most difficult*

You have already met the positive adjectives in this table.

The superlative adjectives all end in –*us*, and have endings like *bonus*.

The comparative adjectives all end in –*ior*. Their endings are like those of *altior*, on the next page:

Comparative adjectives in *–ior*

e.g. fort**ior**, *braver*

	masculine	feminine	neuter
SINGULAR			
nominative	fort**IOR**	fort**IOR**	fort**IUS**
vocative	fort**IOR**	fort**IOR**	fort**IUS**
accusative	fort**IOREM**	fort**IOREM**	fort**IUS**
genitive	fort**IORIS**	fort**IORIS**	fort**IORIS**
dative	fort**IORI**	fort**IORI**	fort**IORI**
ablative	fort**IORE**	fort**IORE**	fort**IORE**
PLURAL			
nominative	fort**IORES**	fort**IORES**	fort**IORA**
vocative	fort**IORES**	fort**IORES**	fort**IORA**
accusative	fort**IORES**	fort**IORES**	fort**IORA**
genitive	fort**IORUM**	fort**IORUM**	fort**IORUM**
dative	fort**IORIBUS**	fort**IORIBUS**	fort**IORIBUS**
ablative	fort**IORIBUS**	fort**IORIBUS**	fort**IORIBUS**

How to say *than*
The Latin word for **than** is *quam*.

Examples:
The boy is wiser than the girl.   *puer est sapientior **quam** puella.*
Girls are wiser than boys.   *puellae sapientiores **quam** pueri sunt.*

Exercise 88.1
1. This soldier is brave. That soldier is braver.
2. That soldier is braver than this soldier.
3. That missile is long. This missile is longer.
4. This missile is longer than that.
5. That girl is wiser than this boy.

Exercise 88.2
1. Teachers are wiser than boys.
2. Teachers are often very wise.
3. This temple is taller than that.
4. This task is not easy but very difficult.
5. Roman soldiers were braver than Greek soldiers.

Exercise 88.3
1. Soldiers are more daring than citizens.
2. Romans were more daring than the Greeks.
3. Greek cities were more beautiful than Roman cities.
4. All women are wiser than men.
5. The Romans were famous, but the Greeks were more famous than the Romans.

Exercise 88.4
1. A very wise man.
2. A very high wall.
3. Very daring soldiers.
4. A very fortunate king.
5. A very cruel master.
6. Very long rivers.
7. A very difficult journey.
8. A very dear wife.
9. A very sacred temple.
10. Very easy tasks.

Exercise 88.5
1. With very happy words.
2. On the higher wall.
3. To the very angry teacher.
4. For the very lucky boys.
5. Of a wiser man.
6. With a more beautiful girl.
7. For the very famous king.
8. Of very cruel masters.
9. For a very long war.
10. By an easier journey.

Exercise 88.6
1. We will not run.
2. The slaves were fortunate.
3. The spears wounded the soldiers.
4. The young men feared the missiles.
5. The journeys are long and difficult.

Exercise 88.7
1. That leader was daring.
2. I have a lucky friend.
3. The leader threw many missiles.
4. Wise men often fear death.
5. Many missiles wounded the leader.

§89 The Story of Troy (Part 14)

Exercise 89.1

Achilles mistreats Hector's body.

1 Achilles vir crudelissimus erat. corpus Hectoris currui suo pedibus vinxit. deinde currum circum muros Troiae egit, corpus Hectoris trahens. omnes cives Troiani, ubi hoc viderunt, 5 tristissimi erant.	currui = dative of currus = chariot pes, pedis m. = foot vincio, -ire, vinxi (4) = I tie circum + acc = around ago, -ere, egi (3) = I drive trahens = dragging
Paris filius Priami erat. frater igitur Hectoris erat. quod Achilles Hectorem occiderat, iratissimus erat. arma cepit, ex urbe cucurrit, in proelium ruit. Achillem mox invenit. haec verba 10 ei dixit:	Priamus, -i m. = Priam (a name) invenio, -ire, inveni (4) = I find
'Achilles, vir pessimus es. nemo peior est quam tu. Hectorem, fratrem meum, occidisti. ego tamen miles melior sum quam tu. numquam effugies. nemo te servare poterit. te 15 nunc occidam.'	pessimus, -a, -um = very wicked peior = more wicked melior = better effugio, -ere, effugi (3¹/₂) = I escape servo, -are, servavi (1) = I save poterit = will be able
Paris telum in Achillem misit. telum in calce Achillis haesit. Achilles ad terram mortuus cecidit.	calx, calcis f. = heel haereo, -ere, haesi (2) = I stick cado, -ere, cecidi (3) = I fall

Exercise 89.2

1. From the passage opposite give, in Latin, one example of each of the following:
   (a) a superlative adjective;
   (b) a preposition;
   (c) a verb in the pluperfect tense;
   (d) an adverb.

2. **occiderat** (line 7).
   (a) Give the Latin subject of this verb.
   (b) Give the Latin object of this verb.

3. **urbe** (line 8).
   (a) In what case is this noun?
   (b) Why is this case used?

4. **misit** (line 16). For this verb, give:
   (a) its tense;
   (b) the first person singular of its present tense.

Vocabulary 45	
around	circum + acc.
I escape	effugio, -ere, effugi (3$\frac{1}{2}$)
I find	invenio, -ire, inveni (4)
I save	servo, -are, -avi (1)

Irregular Comparison of Adjectives

These are very common and must be learned by heart:

Positive	Comparative	Superlative
bonus, *good*	melior, *better*	optimus, *very good, best*
malus, *bad*	peior, *worse*	pessimus, *very bad, worst*
magnus, *big*	maior, *bigger*	maximus, *very big, biggest*
parvus, *small*	minor, *smaller*	minimus, *very small, smallest*
multus, *much, many*	plus, *more*	plurimus, *most, very many*

Have your table of **fortior** (= *braver*) in front of you when doing the following exercise – remember all comparative adjectives ending in *-or* go like this. Beware of the tricky neuter singular ending in *-us*!

Reminder: the superlative adjectives, ending in *-us*, all go like **bonus**. If you don't know how **bonus** goes, why not?!

Exercise 89.3
1. Not all teachers are very good.
2. I have a few very bad boys.
3. We are carrying very big shields.
4. That girl was very small.
5. That ship was very big.

Exercise 89.4
1. I am a good boy, but you (sg) are better.
2. Marcus is the worst boy.
3. Caesar was a very good general.
4. This temple is bigger than that (one).
5. Alexander was a better soldier than Caesar.

Exercise 89.5
1. The food was very good.
2. Very big ships were approaching.
3. She is smaller than you (singular).
4. Italy (=Italia) is bigger than Britain (= Britannia).
5. Britain is smaller than Italy.

Exercise 89.6
1. That girl is very small.
2. This boy is bigger than that girl.
3. Very many soldiers attacked the town.
4. That teacher was the worst.
5. Girls are better than boys.

Exercise 89.7
1. Boys are worse than girls.
2. Roman soldiers were the best.
3. The Romans had better soldiers than the Greeks.
4. The Greeks had worse soldiers than the Romans.
5. Very many citizens were defending the very big town.

Exercise 89.8
1. My wound is very bad.
2. I have never received a worse wound.
3. The mountains of Italy (=Italia) are bigger than the mountains of Britain.
4. The walls of Troy were once very big.
5. The soldiers were in very great danger.

Exercise 89.9
1. This farmer has very many very big fields.
2. In the fields are very many horses.
3. I have never seen a bigger ship than that (one).
4. The Greeks used to build better temples than the Romans.
5. The temples of the Romans were worse than the temples of the Greeks.

§90 The Story of Troy (Part 15); *possum*

Exercise 90.1

The Greeks despair of taking Troy, but Ulysses comes up with a plan.

1 diu Graeci urbem Troiam oppugnaverant. post
multos annos fessi erant. quamquam fortiter
pugnaverant, urbem capere non potuerant.

post + acc = after
annus, -i m. = year

potuerant = they had been able

'quid faciemus?' inquiunt. 'urbem capere non
5 possumus. num Troianos superabimus? muri
Troiae maximi sunt. eos delere numquam
poterimus. domos redire debemus.'

inquiunt = they said
possumus = we are able / can
num = *introduces a question which expects the answer 'no'; surely… not…?*
poterimus = we will be able
domos = to our homes
debeo, -ere, debui + infin (2) = I must, have to, ought to
vox, vocis f. = voice

Ulixes, miles audacissimus Graecorum, ubi
haec verba audivit, iratus erat. magna voce
10 clamavit:

'audite me, Graeci! nolite stulti esse! nos
sapientiores quam Troiani sumus. Troiam mox
capere poterimus. domos redire non debetis!
consilium habeo. consilium optimum habeo.
15 consilio meo urbem capere poterimus. equum
ligneum maximum aedificate!'

nolite + infinitive = don't…!
stultus, -a, -um = stupid

consilium, -i n. = plan

ligneus, -a, -um = wooden

Exercise 90.2

1. From the passage opposite give, in Latin, one example of each of the following:
    (a) a superlative adjective;
    (b) a comparative adjective;
    (c) an imperative;
    (d) an adverb.

2. **urbem** (line 1).
    (a) In what case is this noun?
    (b) Why is this case used?

3. **muri** (line 5).
    What is the case of this noun?

4. **clamavit** (line 10). For this verb, give:
    (a) its person;
    (b) its number;
    (c) its tense.

Vocabulary 46	
after	post + acc.
I am able, I can	possum, posse, potui
voice	vox, vocis f.

Irregular verb: possum, *I am able / I can*

	Present	Imperfect	Perfect	Future	Pluperfect
	can	*could*	*could*	*will be able*	*had been able*
I	possum	poteram	potui	potero	potueram
You (singular)	potes	poteras	potuisti	poteris	potueras
He/She/It	potest	poterat	potuit	poterit	potuerat
We	possumus	poteramus	potuimus	poterimus	potueramus
You (plural)	potestis	poteratis	potuistis	poteritis	potueratis
They	possunt	poterant	potuerunt	poterunt	potuerant
Infinitive *(to be able)*	posse				

This verb will usually have an infinitive (*to*-word) in front of it, to complete the meaning.

Examples

puella <u>currere</u> non potest.
>   *The girl is not able <u>to run</u>.*

=   *The girl cannot run.*

ille miles bene <u>pugnare</u> poterat.
>   *That soldier was able <u>to fight</u> well.*

=   *That soldier could fight well.*

Exercise 90.3

1. I can work.
2. He can escape.
3. We can win.
4. I could not wait.
5. They could flee.

6. I cannot return.
7. We could not run.
8. They were able to attack.
9. I am not able to sleep.
10. You (sg) could not fight.

Exercise 90.4

1. I can read.
2. We could not escape.
3. She cannot laugh.
4. I will not be able to work.
5. He could not attack.

6. I can sail.
7. He could sing.
8. They will be able to come.
9. They could not see.
10. You (pl) can depart.

Exercise 90.5
1. The sailors could sail to the island.
2. We will never be able to beat the enemy.
3. The soldiers were not able to destroy the city.
4. The slaves could not escape from the town.
5. The soldiers will be able to capture this town.

Exercise 90.6
1. The Romans could not throw (their) spears.
2. That king cannot rule well.
3. The citizens were not able to defend the city well.
4. That slave cannot drink this wine.
5. We were not able to come to the city today.

Exercise 90.7
1. Who will be able to come to the temple tomorrow?
2. We will never be able to do this long journey.
3. The soldiers cannot cross this river.
4. The master was not able to set free that slave.
5. The comrades were not able to run quickly.

Exercise 90.8
1. Teachers cannot do everything.
2. The Greeks were not able to beat the Romans in that battle.
3. This man will not be able to write a long book.
4. I was not able to give much money to my son.
5. The tired soldiers were not able to fight well against the enemy.

Exercise 90.9
1. This boy cannot drink wine.
2. The citizens will not be able to defend the town.
3. The soldiers have not been able to do this.
4. The enemy could not find the citizens' money.
5. The leader could not prepare very big forces.

§91 The Story of Troy (Part 16)

Exercise 91.1

The Trojans see the horse.

1 Graeci maximum equum <u>ligneum</u> fecerant. <u>antequam</u> in navibus discesserunt, plurimos milites in equo posuerunt et equum in <u>litore</u> prope urbem <u>reliquerunt</u>.

> ligneus, -a, -um = wooden
> antequam = before
>
> litus, litoris n. = shore
> relinquo, -ere, reliqui (3) = I leave behind, abandon

5 Troiani, ubi hunc equum viderunt, ex urbe exierunt. <u>attoniti</u> erant. diu equum spectaverunt. unus e Troianis 'Graeci' <u>inquit</u> 'discesserunt. <u>nonne</u> eos vicimus? hic equus donum nobis est. eum in <u>mediam</u> urbem
10 <u>trahere</u> <u>debetis</u>, cives!'

> attonitus, -a, -um = amazed
>
> inquit = he said
> nonne = *introduces a question expecting the answer 'yes'.* Surely...?
> medius, -a, -um = middle of
> traho, -ere, traxi (3) = I pull, drag
> debeo, -ere, debui + infin (2) = I must, have to, ought to

Troianus secundus magna voce '<u>num</u>' <u>inquit</u> 'hic equus donum est? Graeci dona numquam dant. <u>homines</u> <u>fallaces</u> sunt. <u>nolite</u> equum in urbem <u>trahere</u>, cives! eum delere <u>debemus</u>!'

> num = *introduces a question expecting the answer 'no'.* Surely... not...?
> homo, hominis m. = man, person; pl: people
> fallax, fallacis = deceitful
> nolite + infin = Do not...!

15 tandem Troiani equum in urbem <u>trahere</u> constituerunt.

Exercise 91.2

1. From the passage opposite give, in Latin, one example of each of the following:
   (a) a verb in the pluperfect tense;
   (b) a preposition;
   (c) an ordinal number;
   (d) an imperative.

2. **equum** (line 1).
   Explain the connection between this word and the English word *equestrian*.

3. **navibus** (line 2).
   (a) In which case is this noun?
   (b) Why is this case used?

4. **posuerunt** (line 3).
   Give the first person singular of the present tense of this verb.

5. **viderunt** (line 5).
   (a) Give the Latin subject of this verb.
   (b) Give the Latin object of this verb.

Vocabulary 47	
before	antequam
do not…!	noli/nolite + infinitive
he said / they said	inquit / inquiunt
I abandon, I leave behind	relinquo, -ere, reliqui (3)
I must, ought to, have to	debeo, -ere, debui + infin (2)
man, person	homo, hominis m./f.
middle of	medius, -a, -um
question expecting *yes*	nonne…?
question expecting *no*	num…?

Prohibitions

Prohibitions are commands telling someone NOT to do something. In English they begin with the words *Do not....*

In Latin singular prohibitions (telling one person not to do something) begin with the word **noli** *(= be unwilling...!).*

Plural prohibitions (telling more than one person not to do something) begin with the word **nolite** *(= be unwilling...!).*

The **noli/nolite** is followed by a present infinitive.

noli currere, puer!   *Do not run, boy!* (singular prohibition)
nolite currere, pueri!   *Do not run, boys!* (plural prohibition)

Reminder: the person being told not to do something will have a VOCATIVE case-ending.

Exercise 91.3
1. Do not fight, slave!
2. Do not fight, slaves!
3. Do not shout, teacher!
4. Do not shout, teachers!
5. Do not sing, girl!
6. Do not sing, girls!
7. Do not drink, young man!
8. Do not drink, young men!
9. Do not flee, friend!
10. Do not flee, friends!

Exercise 91.4
1. Do not listen, master!
2. Do not listen, masters!
3. Do not depart, queen!
4. Do not depart, queens!
5. Do not write, poet!
6. Do not write, poets!
7. Do not enter, farmer!
8. Do not enter, farmers!
9. Do not escape, slave!
10. Do not escape, slaves!

Exercise 91.5
1. Do not laugh, boy!
2. Do not laugh, boys!
3. Do not attack, soldiers!
4. Do not escape, slaves!
5. Do not wait, friend!
6. Do not go in, young man!
7. Do not sail, sailors!
8. Do not be afraid, father!
9. Do not play, girls!
10. Do not depart, mother!

Exercise 91.6

1. Do not run, girls!
2. Do not approach, boy!
3. Do not charge, soldiers!
4. Do not return, friend!
5. Do not work, boys!
6. Do not fight, companions!
7. Do not attack, slave!
8. Do not hurry, mother!
9. Do not reply, boys!
10. Do not fight, citizens!

Exercise 91.7

1. Do not attack the town, soldiers!
2. Do not listen to the teacher's words, boys!
3. Do not write long books, poets!
4. Do not defend the city against the enemy, citizens!
5. Do not punish this slave, master!

Exercise 91.8

1. Do not set free those slaves, masters!
2. Do not go out of the temple, boy!
3. Do not hand over the money to your father, young man!
4. Do not stand in the middle of the road, boys!
5. Do not drink this wine, mother!

Exercise 91.9

1. Do not play in the road, girls!
2. Do not wound the enemy, soldiers!
3. Do not set free this slave, master!
4. Do not cross the river, sailor!
5. Do not listen to that teacher, boys!

Exercise 91.10

1. Do not hand over the money, king!
2. Do not attack the city, Romans!
3. Do not throw your spears, slaves!
4. Do not kill the king, slave!
5. Do not drink all the wine, girl!

§92 Direct Questions: *nonne* and *num*

As you know a Latin sentence can be changed into an open question by adding *–ne* to the end of the <u>first word</u> of the sentence and adding a question mark to the end of the sentence:

Example

laborat.	*He is working.*
labora**tne?**	*Is he working?*

nonne at start of a sentence means that the answer YES is expected. You may need to give some thought to how to express this in good English.

Examples

nonne laborat?	*He <u>is</u> working, isn't he?*
nonne ridebas?	*You were laughing, weren't you?*

num at the start of a sentence means that the answer NO is expected.

Examples

num laborat?	*He isn't working, is he?*
num ridebas?	*You weren't laughing, were you?*

(In some dictionaries and word lists you will see nonne *translated as 'surely?' and* num *translated as 'surely not?'. This gives a rough idea of what's going on, but these aren't really the meanings of these words. Besides, using 'surely' or 'surely not' will often end up sounding like bad English. Try to avoid using 'surely' and 'surely not' if you can, and follow the pattern of the English examples above).*

Exercise 92.1

1. We are shouting.
2. We are shouting, aren't we?
3. We are not shouting, are we?
4. He is running.
5. He is running, isn't he?
6. He isn't running, is he?
7. They are laughing.
8. They aren't laughing, are they?
9. They are laughing, aren't they?
10. He's a bad boy, isn't he?

Exercise 92.2
1. He wasn't fighting well, was he?
2. He was fighting well, wasn't he?
3. This soldier is brave, isn't he?
4. This soldier isn't brave, is he?
5. Hector was a bold soldier, wasn't he?

Exercise 92.3
1. Achilles wasn't a brave soldier, was he?
2. Hector was the bravest, wasn't he?
3. We are Romans, aren't we?
4. We aren't Romans, are we?
5. You (sg) are not shouting, are you?

Exercise 92.4
1. He was laughing, wasn't he?
2. He was not laughing, was he?
3. The soldiers were not bold, were they?
4. They will not escape, will they?
5. You (sg) are running, aren't you?

Exercise 92.5
1. The citizens were defending the city well, weren't they?
2. The boy didn't do this, did he?
3. Surely the Greeks didn't beat the Romans?
4. You (sg) love your mother, don't you?
5. The Greeks collected many weapons, didn't they?

Exercise 92.6
1. A woman will not be able to do this, will she?
2. The Roman soldiers fought well in the battle, didn't they?
3. It isn't difficult to do this, is it?
4. This man is not very wise, is he?
5. That journey will not be easy, will it?

§93 *debeo* – I must, have to, ought to

Like the verb *possum* (I can, I am able), the verb *debeo* will have an infinitive (a *to*-word, usually ending in *-re*) just in front of it to complete the sense.

Examples
effugere debemus.   *We must (**or** have to, **or** ought to) escape.*
hoc mox facere debebis.   *You will have to do this soon.*

Exercise 93.1
1. You (sg) ought to work.
2. We must hurry.
3. They will have to run.
4. He ought to fight.
5. You (pl) must listen.
6. They had to escape.
7. I must go.
8. You (sg) ought to sleep.
9. She ought to stay.
10. He will have to go.

Exercise 93.2
1. The slaves had to escape.
2. Boys ought not to play.
3. Girls ought not to cry.
4. The poet must write.
5. We must attack immediately.

Exercise 93.3
1. The enemy had to capture the city.
2. The old man ought to arrive soon.
3. Soldiers have to run quickly.
4. This young man ought to drink good wine.
5. Teachers ought not to frighten (their) pupils.

Exercise 93.4
1. Kings and queens ought to rule well.
2. Masters ought not to punish slaves.
3. That teacher ought to warn the boys and girls.
4. Poets ought to write good books.
5. Soldiers must build walls well.

§94 The Story of Troy (Part 17)

Exercise 94.1

The Fall of Troy

1 Troiani equum in urbem <u>traxerunt</u>. laetissimi erant quod Graeci discesserant. laetissimi erant quod Graecos vicerant.

traho, -ere, traxi (3) = I drag

illa <u>nocte</u> igitur omnes cives multum cibi
5 consumebant et multum vini bibebant. mox omnes Troiani dormiebant.

nox, noctis f. = night

media <u>nocte</u> milites Graeci, <u>qui</u> in equo erant, de equo <u>silentio</u> <u>descenderunt</u>. subito ad Troianos <u>dormientes</u> magnis <u>clamoribus</u>
10 <u>ruerunt</u>. Troiani <u>se</u> defendere non poterant. multi Troiani gladiis Graecorum perierunt. inter hos erat Priamus <u>senex</u>, rex Troiae. Graeci <u>paucos</u> Troianos <u>vivos</u> reliquerunt.

qui = who
silentio = in silence
descendo, -ere, descendi (3) = I climb down
dormientes = as they were sleeping
clamor, -oris m. = shout
se = themselves
senex, senis m. = old man
pauci, -ae, -a = few
vivus, -a, -um = alive

sic Graeci post decem <u>annos</u> urbem Troiam
15 <u>dolo</u> ceperunt. maximam <u>partem</u> urbis deleverunt. Helenam ad <u>Graeciam</u> <u>reducere</u> iam poterant.

annus, -i m. = year
dolus, -i m. = trickery
pars, partis f. = part
Graecia, -ae f. = Greece
reduco, -ere, reduxi (3) = I lead back

Exercise 94.2

1. From the passage on the previous page give, in Latin, one example of each of the following:
    (a) a superlative adjective;
    (b) a verb in the imperfect tense;
    (c) a preposition followed by a noun in the accusative case;
    (d) an infinitive.

2. **vicerant** (line 3).
    For this verb, give:
    (a) its person;
    (b) its number;
    (c) its tense;
    (d) the first person singular of its present tense.

3.
    urbem (line 14).
    (a) In what case is this noun?
    (b) Why is this case used?

Vocabulary 48	
alive	vivus, -a, -um
few	pauci, -ae, -a (plural endings)
himself	se
I lead back	reduco, -ere, reduxi (3)
old man	senex, senis m.
part	pars, partis f.
shout	clamor, clamoris m.

Third Person Reflexive Pronoun: *se*

	singular		*plural*	
nominative	(cannot exist)		(cannot exist)	
accusative	se	*himself/herself*	se	*themselves*
genitive	sui	*of himself/herself*	sui	*of themselves*
dative	sibi	*to/for himself/herself*	sibi	*to/for themselves*
ablative	se	*(by) himself/herself*	se	*(by) themselves*
note:	secum	*with him / with her*	secum	*with them*

Summary of Reflexive Pronouns

singular		*plural*	
me	*myself*	nos	*ourselves*
te	*yourself*	vos	*yourselves*
se	*himself/herself/itself*	se	*themselves*

Exercise 94.3
1. That boy likes himself.
2. We never praise ourselves.
3. The Trojans prepared to defend themselves.
4. That girl is always looking at herself.
5. Wise boys never praise themselves.

Exercise 94.4
1. The Romans decided to kill themselves.
2. The citizens were defending themselves bravely.
3. The slaves wanted to save themselves.
4. That girl wounded herself with a sword.
5. The citizens handed themselves over to the enemy.

Exercise 94.5
1. Why are we not defending ourselves?
2. The old man wanted to kill himself.
3. I saw myself in the river.
4. Why did you wound yourselves?
5. They took the money for themselves.

Exercise 94.6
1. The father ordered his son to go with him.
2. We shall always defend ourselves bravely.
3. The slaves were fighting among themselves.
4. The sad citizens decided to kill themselves.
5. Boy, why are you always praising yourself?

Summary of Grammar and Syntax

Contents

97

SECTION 1: Grammatical Terms

adjectives	These are words that describe nouns. e.g. *bonus* (good), *tristis* (sad).
adverbs	These are words which describe verbs. e.g. *celeriter* (quickly), *statim* (immediately)
cardinal number	*unus* (one), *duo* (two), *tres* (three) etc. Note carefully the difference between this and an ORDINAL NUMBER.
case	nominative (subject), vocative (person spoken to), accusative (object), genitive (of), dative (to or for) or ablative (by, with, from).
comparative adjective	An adjective ending in *–or* meaning 'more....' e.g. *pulchrior* (more beautiful).
conjugation	A family of verbs. e.g. *amo* (1) is in the first conjugation; *audio* (4) is in the fourth conjugation.
conjunction	A joining word. e.g. *et* (and), *sed* (but).
declension	A family of nouns. e.g. *puella* (girl) in in the first declension; *servus* (slave) is in the second declension; *rex* (king) is in the third declension.
gender	Whether a noun or adjective is masculine, feminine or neuter.
imperative	An order. e.g. *audi!* (listen!), *amate!* (love!).
infinitive	A *to* word, the second principal part of a verb, usually ending in *–re* in Latin. e.g. *amare* (to love). But beware of *esse* (to be).
number	Whether a noun or verb is SINGULAR or PLURAL.
ordinal number	*primus* (first), *secundus* (second), *tertius* (third) and so on. Note carefully the difference between this an a CARDINAL NUMBER.

person	1st person singular = I
	2nd person singular = You
	3rd person singular = He, She, It
	1st person plural = We
	2nd person plural = You
	3rd person plural = They
positive adjective	A 'normal' adjective, like *bonus* (good), *pulcher* (beautiful) or *tristis* (sad). See also COMPARATIVE ADJECTIVE and SUPERLATIVE ADJECTIVE.
prepositions	Little words like *cum* (with), *ad* (to, towards), *in* (in). In Latin, some prepositions are followed by accusative nouns, others by ablative nouns. See Section 5 in this guide, and Section 41 of your purple vocabulary booklet.
relative pronoun	The *qui, quae, quod* (*who, which* etc) table.
superlative adjective	An adjective ending in *-issimus* or *-errimus*, meaning 'very' or 'most'. e.g. *tristissimus* (very sad), *pulcherrimus* (most beautiful).
tense	Present, future, imperfect, perfect or pluperfect.

SECTION 2 - NOUNS

2.1 Summary of case usage

name of case	job	examples
nominative	subject (doer) of verb	**servus** laborat. *The slave is working.*
	with the verb *to be*	Marcus est **servus**. *Marcus is a slave.*
vocative	person spoken to	**serve**, quid facis? *Slave, what are you doing?*
accusative	object (receiver) of verb	**servum** punio. *I am punishing the slave.*
	after prepositions like *ad, per*	ad **servum** currit. *He is running towards the slave.*
genitive	'of'	dominus **servi** est saevus. *The master of the slave is cruel.*
dative	'to', 'for'	pecuniam **servo** dat. *He gives money to the slave.*
ablative	'by', 'with', 'from'	puerum **gladio** vulnerat. *He wounds the boy with his sword.*
	after prepositions like *cum, in*	cum **servo** pugnat. *He is fighting with the slave.*

2.2 Summary of Nouns

Declension:	1	2	2	2	2
Gender:	*f*	*m*	*m*	*m*	*n*
	girl	*slave*	*boy*	*field*	*war*
SINGULAR					
nominative	puell**A**	serv**US**	pu**ER**	ag**ER**	bell**UM**
vocative	puell**A**	serv**E**	pu**ER**	ag**ER**	bell**UM**
accusative	puell**AM**	serv**UM**	puer**UM**	agr**UM**	bell**UM**
genitive	puell**AE**	serv**I**	puer**I**	agr**I**	bell**I**
dative	puell**AE**	serv**O**	puer**O**	agr**O**	bell**O**
ablative	puell**A**	serv**O**	puer**O**	agr**O**	bell**O**
PLURAL	*girls*	*slaves*	*boys*	*fields*	*wars*
nominative	puell**AE**	serv**I**	puer**I**	agr**I**	bell**A**
vocative	puell**AE**	serv**I**	puer**I**	agr**I**	bell**A**
accusative	puell**AS**	serv**OS**	puer**OS**	agr**OS**	bell**A**
genitive	puell**ARUM**	serv**ORUM**	puer**ORUM**	agr**ORUM**	bell**ORUM**
dative	puell**IS**	serv**IS**	puer**IS**	agr**IS**	bell**IS**
ablative	puell**IS**	serv**IS**	puer**IS**	agr**IS**	bell**IS**

Declension:	3	3
Gender:	*m/f*	*n*
	king (m.)	*task*
SINGULAR		
nominative	rex	opus
vocative	rex	opus
accusative	reg**EM**	opus
genitive	reg**IS**	oper**IS**
dative	reg**I**	oper**I**
ablative	reg**E**	oper**E**
PLURAL	*kings*	*tasks*
nominative	reg**ES**	oper**A**
vocative	reg**ES**	oper**A**
accusative	reg**ES**	oper**A**
genitive	reg**UM**	oper**UM**
dative	reg**IBUS**	oper**IBUS**
ablative	reg**IBUS**	oper**IBUS**

SECTION 3 - ADJECTIVES

3.1 Adjectives in *–us*

e.g. bon**US**, *good*

	masculine	feminine	neuter
SINGULAR			
nominative	bon**US**	bon**A**	bon**UM**
vocative	bon**E**	bon**A**	bon**UM**
accusative	bon**UM**	bon**AM**	bon**UM**
genitive	bon**I**	bon**AE**	bon**I**
dative	bon**O**	bon**AE**	bon**O**
ablative	bon**O**	bon**A**	bon**O**
PLURAL			
nominative	bon**I**	bon**AE**	bon**A**
vocative	bon**I**	bon**AE**	bon**A**
accusative	bon**OS**	bon**AS**	bon**A**
genitive	bon**ORUM**	bon**ARUM**	bon**ORUM**
dative	bon**IS**	bon**IS**	bon**IS**
ablative	bon**IS**	bon**IS**	bon**IS**

3.2 Adjectives in *–er* (keeping the *e)*

e.g. mis**ER**, *miserable*

	masculine	feminine	neuter
SINGULAR			
nominative	miser	miser**A**	miser**UM**
vocative	miser	miser**A**	miser**UM**
accusative	miser**UM**	miser**AM**	miser**UM**
genitive	miser**I**	miser**AE**	miser**I**
dative	miser**O**	miser**AE**	miser**O**
ablative	miser**O**	miser**A**	miser**O**
PLURAL			
nominative	miser**I**	miser**AE**	miser**A**
vocative	miser**I**	miser**AE**	miser**A**
accusative	miser**OS**	miser**AS**	miser**A**
genitive	miser**ORUM**	miser**ARUM**	miser**ORUM**
dative	miser**IS**	miser**IS**	miser**IS**
ablative	miser**IS**	miser**IS**	miser**IS**

3.3 Adjectives in –er (dropping the e)

e.g. pulchER, *beautiful*

	masculine	feminine	neuter
SINGULAR			
nominative	pulcher	pulchrA	pulchrUM
vocative	pulcher	pulchrA	pulchrUM
accusative	pulchrUM	pulchrAM	pulchrUM
genitive	pulchrI	pulchrAE	pulchrI
dative	pulchrO	pulchrAE	pulchrO
ablative	pulchrO	pulchrA	pulchrO
PLURAL			
nominative	pulchrI	pulchrAE	pulchrA
vocative	pulchrI	pulchrAE	pulchrA
accusative	pulchrOS	pulchrAS	pulchrA
genitive	pulchrORUM	pulchrARUM	pulchrORUM
dative	pulchrIS	pulchrIS	pulchrIS

3.4 Third Declension Adjectives in –is

e.g. fortIS, *brave, strong*

	masculine	feminine	neuter
SINGULAR			
nominative	fortIS	fortIS	fortE
vocative	fortIS	fortIS	fortE
accusative	fortEM	fortEM	fortE
genitive	fortIS	fortIS	fortIS
dative	fortI	fortI	fortI
ablative	fortI	fortI	fortI
PLURAL			
nominative	fortES	fortES	fortIA
vocative	fortES	fortES	fortIA
accusative	fortES	fortES	fortIA
genitive	fortIUM	fortIUM	fortIUM
dative	fortIBUS	fortIBUS	fortIBUS
ablative	fortIBUS	fortIBUS	fortIBUS

3.5 Third Declension Adjectives in –x

e.g. feli**X**, *fortunate*

	masculine	feminine	neuter
SINGULAR			
nominative	felix	felix	felix
vocative	felix	felix	felix
accusative	felic**EM**	felic**EM**	felix
genitive	felic**IS**	felic**IS**	felic**IS**
dative	felic**I**	felic**I**	felic**I**
ablative	felic**I**	felic**I**	felic**I**
PLURAL			
nominative	felic**ES**	felic**ES**	felic**IA**
vocative	felic**ES**	felic**ES**	felic**IA**
accusative	felic**ES**	felic**ES**	felic**IA**
genitive	felic**IUM**	felic**IUM**	felic**IUM**
dative	felic**IBUS**	felic**IBUS**	felic**IBUS**
ablative	felic**IBUS**	felic**IBUS**	felic**IBUS**

3.6 Third Declension Adjectives in –ns

e.g. inge**ns**, *huge*

	masculine	feminine	neuter
SINGULAR			
nominative	ingens	ingens	ingens
vocative	ingens	ingens	ingens
accusative	ingent**EM**	ingent**EM**	ingens
genitive	ingent**IS**	ingent**IS**	ingent**IS**
dative	ingent**I**	ingent**I**	ingent**I**
ablative	ingent**I**	ingent**I**	ingent**I**
PLURAL			
nominative	ingent**ES**	ingent**ES**	ingent**IA**
vocative	ingent**ES**	ingent**ES**	ingent**IA**
accusative	ingent**ES**	ingent**ES**	ingent**IA**
genitive	ingent**IUM**	ingent**IUM**	ingent**IUM**
dative	ingent**IBUS**	ingent**IBUS**	ingent**IBUS**
ablative	ingent**IBUS**	ingent**IBUS**	ingent**IBUS**

3.7 Comparison in Latin

Here are some examples:

	Positive	Comparative	Superlative
-us		**STEM + IOR**	**STEM + ISSIMUS**
	altus *high*	altior *higher*	altissimus *highest/very high*
-er		**STEM + IOR**	**POSITIVE + RIMUS**
	miser *miserable*	miserior *more miserable*	miserrimus *very miserable*
	pulcher *beautiful*	pulchrior *more beautiful*	pulcherrimus *very beautiful*
-is		**STEM + IOR**	**STEM + ISSIMUS**
	fortis *brave*	fortior *more brave*	fortissimus *very brave, the bravest*
-x	felix *fortunate*	felicior *more fortunate*	felicissimus *very fortunate*
-ns	ingens *huge*	ingentior *more huge*	ingentissimus *very huge*

3.8 Comparative adjectives in *–ior*

e.g. fort**ior**, *braver*

	masculine	feminine	neuter
SINGULAR			
nominative	fort**IOR**	fort**IOR**	fort**IUS**
vocative	fort**IOR**	fort**IOR**	fort**IUS**
accusative	fort**IOREM**	fort**IOREM**	fort**IUS**
genitive	fort**IORIS**	fort**IORIS**	fort**IORIS**
dative	fort**IORI**	fort**IORI**	fort**IORI**
ablative	fort**IORE**	fort**IORE**	fort**IORE**
PLURAL			
nominative	fort**IORES**	fort**IORES**	fort**IORA**
vocative	fort**IORES**	fort**IORES**	fort**IORA**
accusative	fort**IORES**	fort**IORES**	fort**IORA**
genitive	fort**IORUM**	fort**IORUM**	fort**IORUM**
dative	fort**IORIBUS**	fort**IORIBUS**	fort**IORIBUS**
ablative	fort**IORIBUS**	fort**IORIBUS**	fort**IORIBUS**

• 3.9 Irregular Comparison of Adjectives

Positive	Comparative	Superlative
bonus, *good*	melior, *better*	optimus, *very good, best*
malus, *bad*	peior, *worse*	pessimus, *very bad, worst*
magnus, *big*	maior, *bigger*	maximus, *very big, biggest*
parvus, *small*	minor, *smaller*	minimus, *very small, smallest*
multus, *much, many*	plus, *more*	plurimus, *most, very many*

SECTION 4 – PRONOUNS

4.1 First Person Pronoun: *ego*

	singular		*plural*	
nominative	ego	*I*	nos	*we*
accusative	me	*me*	nos	*us*
genitive	mei	*of me/my*	nostrum	*of us/our*
dative	mihi	*to/for me*	nobis	*to/for us*
ablative	me	*(by) me*	nobis	*(by) us*
note:	mecum	*with me*	nobiscum	*with us*

4.2 Second Person Pronoun: *tu*

	singular		*plural*	
nominative	tu	*you*	vos	*you*
accusative	te	*you*	vos	*you*
genitive	tui	*of you/your*	vestrum	*of you/your*
dative	tibi	*to/for you*	vobis	*to/for you*
ablative	te	*(by) you*	vobis	*(by) you*
note:	tecum	*with you*	vobiscum	*with you*

4.3 Third Person Reflexive Pronoun: *se*

	singular		*plural*	
nominative		-		-
accusative	se	*himself/herself*	se	*themselves*
genitive	sui	*of himself/herself*	sui	*of themselves*
dative	sibi	*to/for himself/herself*	sibi	*to/for themselves*
ablative	se	*(by) himself/herself*	se	*(by) themselves*
note:	secum	*with him / with her*	secum	*with them*

4.4 Demonstrative adjective: hic, haec, hoc = *'this'* (plural: *'these'*)

'Demonstrative' just means 'pointing something out'. The word *this* points to something near the speaker.

	masculine	feminine	neuter
SINGULAR			
nominative	hic	haec	hoc
accusative	hunc	hanc	hoc
genitive	huius	huius	huius
dative	huic	huic	huic
ablative	hoc	hac	hoc
PLURAL			
nominative	hi	hae	haec
accusative	hos	has	haec
genitive	horum	harum	horum
dative	his	his	his
ablative	his	his	his

4.5 Demonstrative adjective: ille, illa, illud = 'that' (plural: 'those')

'Demonstrative' just means 'pointing something out'. The word *that* points to something at a distance from the speaker.

	masculine	feminine	neuter
SINGULAR			
nominative	ille	illa	illud
accusative	illum	illam	illud
genitive	illius	illius	illius
dative	illi	illi	illi
ablative	illo	illa	illo
PLURAL			
nominative	illi	illae	illa
accusative	illos	illas	illa
genitive	illorum	illarum	illorum
dative	illis	illis	illis
ablative	illis	illis	illis

4.6 Third Person Pronoun: *is, ea, id (= he, she, it)*

	masculine		feminine		neuter	
SINGULAR						
nominative	is	*he*	ea	*she*	id	*it*
accusative	eum	*him*	eam	*her*	id	*it*
genitive	eius	*his*	eius	*her*	eius	*of it*
dative	ei	*to him*	ei	*to her*	ei	*to it*
ablative	eo	*by him*	ea	*by her*	eo	*by it*
PLURAL						
nominative	ei	*they*	eae	*they*	ea	*they*
accusative	eos	*them*	eas	*them*	ea	*them*
genitive	eorum	*their*	earum	*their*	eorum	*their*
dative	eis	*to them*	eis	*to them*	eis	*to them*
ablative	eis	*by them*	eis	*by them*	eis	*by them*

SECTION 5 - PREPOSITIONS

5.1 Level 1

ad + accusative	*to, towards*	ad reginam ambulat. *He is walking towards the queen.*
contra + accusative	*against*	contra nautam pugnat. *He is fighting against the sailor.*
per + accusative	*through, along*	per viam currit. *He is running along the road.*
prope + accusative	*near*	prope murum stat. *He is standing near the wall.*
trans + accusative	*across*	trans viam festinat. *He hurries across the road.*
a/ab + ablative	(*away*) *from*	ab insula navigat. *He sails away from the island.*
cum + ablative	*with*	cum amico ludit. *He is playing with a friend.*
de + ablative	*down from, about*	de periculo monet. *He warns about the danger.*
e/ex + ablative	*out of*	ex oppido currit. *He runs out of the town.*

5.2 The Preposition *in*

This frequently causes problems, because it can be followed by an ablative word (when it means *in* or *on*.) as well as by an accusative word (when it means *into*).

Examples

in + ablative = *in*.   equus in ag**ro** currit.
                         *The horse is running **in** the field.*

in + accusative = *into*.   equus in ag**rum** currit.
                             *The horse is running **into** the field.*

5.3 Level 2

ante + accusative	*before*	ante tempestatem timet. *He is afraid before the storm.*
circum + accusative	*around*	circum insulam navigat. *He sails around the island.*
inter + accusative	*among, between*	inter equos currit. *He runs between the horses.*
post + accusative	*after, behind*	post patrem ambulat. *He is walking behind his father.*
propter + accusative	*because of*	propter pericula fugit. *He flees because of the dangers.*
super + accusative	*above*	super aquam stat. *He is standing above the water.*
pro + ablative	*on behalf of, for, in front of*	pro domino pugnat. *He fights for his master.*
sine + ablative	*without*	sine gladio pugnat. *He is fighting without a sword.*
sub + ablative	*under*	sub equo dormit. *He is sleeping under the horse.*

SECTION 6 – VERBS

6.1 Present Tense

	1	2	3	4	3¹/₂ / M
	love	*warn*	*rule*	*hear*	*take*
I	am**O**	mon**EO**	reg**O**	aud**IO**	cap**IO**
You (sing.)	am**AS**	mon**ES**	reg**IS**	aud**IS**	cap**IS**
He/She/It	am**AT**	mon**ET**	reg**IT**	aud**IT**	cap**IT**
We	am**AMUS**	mon**EMUS**	reg**IMUS**	aud**IMUS**	cap**IMUS**
You (pl.)	am**ATIS**	mon**ETIS**	reg**ITIS**	aud**ITIS**	cap**ITIS**
They	am**ANT**	mon**ENT**	reg**UNT**	aud**IUNT**	cap**IUNT**

6.2 Imperfect Tense

	1	2	4	3¹/₂ / M
	loving	*warning*	*hearing*	*taking*
I was...	am**ABAM**	mon**EBAM**	aud**IEBAM**	cap**IEBAM**
You were...	am**ABAS**	mon**EBAS**	aud**IEBAS**	cap**IEBAS**
He/She/It was...	am**ABAT**	mon**EBAT**	aud**IEBAT**	cap**IEBAT**
We were...	am**ABAMUS**	mon**EBAMUS**	aud**IEBAMUS**	cap**IEBAMUS**
You were...	am**ABATIS**	mon**EBATIS**	aud**IEBATIS**	cap**IEBATIS**
They were...	am**ABANT**	mon**EBANT**	aud**IEBANT**	cap**IEBANT**

6.3 Perfect Tense

	1	2	3	4	3¹/₂ / M
	loved	*warned*	*ruled*	*heard*	*took*
I	amav**I**	monu**I**	rex**I**	audiv**I**	cep**I**
You	amav**ISTI**	monu**ISTI**	rex**ISTI**	audiv**ISTI**	cep**ISTI**
He/She/It	amav**IT**	monu**IT**	rex**IT**	audiv**IT**	cep**IT**
We	amav**IMUS**	monu**IMUS**	rex**IMUS**	audiv**IMUS**	cep**IMUS**
You	amav**ISTIS**	monu**ISTIS**	rex**ISTIS**	audiv**ISTIS**	cep**ISTIS**
They	amav**ERUNT**	monu**ERUNT**	rex**ERUNT**	audiv**ERUNT**	cep**ERUNT**

6.4 Future Tense

	1	2	3	4	3¹/₂ / M
	love	*warn*	*rule*	*hear*	*take*
I will	ama**BO**	mone**BO**	reg**AM**	audi**AM**	capi**AM**
You (sing.) will	ama**BIS**	mone**BIS**	reg**ES**	audi**ES**	capi**ES**
He/She/It will	ama**BIT**	mone**BIT**	reg**ET**	audi**ET**	capi**ET**
We will	ama**BIMUS**	mone**BIMUS**	reg**EMUS**	audi**EMUS**	capi**EMUS**
You (pl.) will	ama**BITIS**	mone**BITIS**	reg**ETIS**	audi**ETIS**	capi**ETIS**
They will	ama**BUNT**	mone**BUNT**	reg**ENT**	audi**ENT**	capi**ENT**

6.5 Pluperfect Tense

	1	2	3	4	3¹/₂ / M
	loved	*warned*	*ruled*	*heard*	*taken*
I had	amav**ERAM**	monu**ERAM**	rex**ERAM**	audiv**ERAM**	cep**ERAM**
You (sing.) had	amav**ERAS**	monu**ERAS**	rex**ERAS**	audiv**ERAS**	cep**ERAS**
He/She/It had	amav**ERAT**	monu**ERAT**	rex**ERAT**	audiv**ERAT**	cep**ERAT**
We had	amav**ERAMUS**	monu**ERAMUS**	rex**ERAMUS**	audiv**ERAMUS**	cep**ERAMUS**
You (pl.) had	amav**ERATIS**	monu**ERATIS**	rex**ERATIS**	audiv**ERATIS**	cep**ERATIS**
They had	amav**ERANT**	monu**ERANT**	rex**ERANT**	audiv**ERANT**	cep**ERANT**

6.6 Present Infinitives

Conjugation	*Present*	*English*	*Infinitive*	*English*
1	amo	*I love*	am**ARE**	*to love*
2	moneo	*I warn*	mon**ERE**	*to warn*
3	rego	*I rule*	reg**ERE**	*to rule*
4	audio	*I hear*	aud**IRE**	*to hear*
3¹/₂ / M	capio	*I take*	cap**ERE**	*to take*
irregular verb	sum	*I am*	esse	*to be*

6.7 Imperatives

Conjugation	*singular*	*plural*	*English*
1	am**A**	am**ATE**	*Love!*
2	mon**E**	mon**ETE**	*Warn!*
3	reg**E**	reg**ITE**	*Rule!*
4	aud**I**	aud**ITE**	*Hear!/Listen!*
3¹/₂ / M	cap**E**	cap**ITE**	*Take!*
sum	es	este	*Be!*

6.8 Irregular verb: sum, *I am*

	Present	Imperfect	Perfect	Future	Pluperfect
	am/are/is	*was/were*	*was/were*	*will be*	*had been*
I	sum	eram	fui	ero	fueram
You (singular)	es	eras	fuisti	eris	fueras
He/She/It	est	erat	fuit	erit	fuerat
We	sumus	eramus	fuimus	erimus	fueramus
You (plural)	estis	eratis	fuistis	eritis	fueratis
They	sunt	erant	fuerunt	erunt	fuerant

Infinitive ('to')	esse
Imperatives ('be!')	
singular:	es
plural:	este

6.9 Irregular verb: possum, *I am able/I can*

	Present	Imperfect	Perfect	Future	Pluperfect
	can	*could*	*could*	*will be able*	*had been able*
I	possum	poteram	potui	potero	potueram
You (singular)	potes	poteras	potuisti	poteris	potueras
He/She/It	potest	poterat	potuit	poterit	potuerat
We	possumus	poteramus	potuimus	poterimus	potueramus
You (plural)	potestis	poteratis	potuistis	poteritis	potueratis
They	possunt	poterant	potuerunt	poterunt	potuerant

Infinitive ('to')	posse

6.10 Irregular verb: *eo, I go*

	Present	Imperfect	Perfect	Future	Pluperfect
	go	*was/were going*	*went*	*will go*	*had gone*
I	eo	ibam	ii / ivi	ibo	ieram / iveram
You (singular)	is	ibas	iisti / ivisti	ibis	ieras / iveras
He/She/It	it	ibat	iit / ivit	ibit	ierat / iverat
We	imus	ibamus	iimus / ivimus	ibimus	ieramus / iveramus
You (plural)	itis	ibatis	iistis / ivistis	ibitis	ieratis / iveratis
They	eunt	ibant	ierunt / iverunt	ibunt	ierant / iverant

Infinitive ('to')	ire
Imperatives	
singular:	i
plural:	ite

SECTION 7 – SYNTAX

7.1 Adverbs
Adverbs do not change their form in Latin. They will usually be found just before the verb at the end of the sentence.

servi <u>fortiter</u> pugnant.   *The slaves fight bravely.*
pueri <u>semper</u> <u>bene</u> laborant.   *Boys always work well.*

7.2 *quod* (= because) clauses
These are straightforward:

puella nautam amabat <u>quod</u> pecuniam habebat.
The girl liked the sailor <u>because</u> he had money.

servi, <u>quod</u> dominum timebant, fugerunt.
<u>Because</u> the slaves were afraid of their master, they fled.

7.3 ubi *(= when)* clauses
These also are straighforward:

<u>ubi</u> magistrum vidit, perterritus erat.
<u>When</u> he saw the teacher, he was frightened.

servi, <u>ubi</u> pericula viderunt, cucurrerunt.
<u>When</u> the slaves saw the dangers, they ran.

7.4 Direct Questions: *-ne*
A Latin statement can be changed into a question be adding *–ne* to the end of the <u>first word</u> of the sentence and adding a question mark to the end of the sentence:

<u>Examples</u>

1.	laborat.	*He is working.*
	laborat**ne?**	*Is he working?*
2.	est fessus.	*He is tired.*
	est**ne** fessus?	*Is he tired?*
3.	puer puellam spectat.	*The boy is looking at the girl.*
	puer**ne** puellam spectat?	*Is the boy looking at the girl?*

7.5 Present infinitives

You will find present infinitives used with the verbs *prepare* (**paro**), *want* (**cupio**), *decide* (**constituo**) and *order* (**iubeo**). The infinitive usually comes just before the main verb at the end of the sentence.

puella <u>cantare</u> parat.	*The girl prepares <u>to sing</u>.*
pueri <u>ludere</u> cupiunt.	*The boys want <u>to work</u>.*
servi <u>pugnare</u> constituerunt.	*The slaves decided <u>to fight</u>.*
dominus servos bene <u>laborare</u> iussit.	*The master ordered the slaves <u>to work</u>.*

7.6 quamquam (=*although*) clauses

These are straightforward:

quamquam femina pecuniam habebat, virum non habebat.
Although the woman had money, she did not have a husband.

milites, quamquam fessi erant, bene pugnaverunt.
Although the soldiers were tired, they fought well.

7.7 Comparisons with quam (=*than*)

quam (*than*) is used to compare things.

hic miles clarior quam ille erat.
This soldier was more famous <u>than</u> that one.

puellae sapientiores quam pueri sunt.
Girls are wiser <u>than</u> boys.

7.8 Direct Questions: *nonne* and *num*.

nonne can be added to the start of a sentence to indicate that the answer 'yes' is expected. How you actually translate this word will depend on the sentence.

<u>Example</u>	nonne laborat?	*He is working, isn't he?*
		Surely he is working?

num can be added to the start of a sentence to indicate that the answer 'no' is expected. How you actually translate this word will depend on the sentence.

<u>Example</u>	num laborat?	*He is not working, is he?*
		Surely he is not working?

7.9 Prohibitions

Prohibitions are commands telling someone NOT to do something. In English they begin with the words *Do not....*

In Latin singular prohibitions (telling one person not to do something) begin with the word **noli**.

Plural prohibitions (telling more than one person not to do something) begin with the word **nolite**.

The **noli/nolite** is followed by a present infinitive.

noli currere, puer!	*Do not run, boy!* (singular prohibition)
nolite currere, pueri!	*Do not run, boys!* (plural prohibition)

7.10 Reflexive Pronouns

These are pronouns which reflect ('bend back') the action to the subject.

<u>me</u> cras necabo.
I shall kill <u>myself</u> tomorrow.

ille puer <u>se</u> amat.
That boy likes <u>himself</u>.

cur <u>vos</u> non defenditis, milites?
Why are you not defending yourselves, soldiers?

cives <u>se</u> hostibus tradiderunt.
The citizens handed themsleves over to the enemy.

SECTION 8 – NUMERALS

8.1 Cardinal numbers 1-20

unus	one
duo	two
tres	three
quattuor	four
quinque	five
sex	six
septem	seven
octo	eight
novem	nine
decem	ten

undecim	eleven
duodecim	twelve
tredecim	thirteen
quattuordecim	fourteen
quindecim	fifteen
sedecim	sixteen
septendecim	seventeen
duodeviginti	eighteen
undeviginti	nineteen
viginti	twenty

8.2 Ordinal numbers 1st – 10th

primus	first
secundus	second
tertius	third
quartus	fourth
quintus	fifth
sextus	sixth
septimus	seventh
octavus	eighth
nonus	ninth
decimus	tenth

Vocabulary: Latin-English

a/ab + ablative	*from, by*
absum, abesse, afui (irreg.)	*be away*
accipio, -ere, accepi $3\frac{1}{2}$	*receive*
ad + accusative	*to, towards*
adeo (adverb)	*so, to such an extent*
adeo, adire, adii (irreg.)	*go towards*
adfu-	*see adsum*
adsum, adesse, adfui (irreg.)	*be present*
advenio, -ire, adveni 4	*arrive*
aedifico, -are, -avi 1	*build*
afu-	*see absum*
ager, agri 2 m.	*field*
ago, -ere, egi 3	*do*
agricola, -ae 1 m.	*farmer*
alius	*other*
altus, -a, -um	*high, deep*
ambulo, -are, -avi 1	*walk*
amicus, -i 2 m.	*friend*
amo, -are, -avi 1	*love, like*
ancilla, -ae 1 f.	*maidservant*
ante + accusative	*before; in front of*
antequam	*before*
appropinquo, -are, -avi 1	*approach*
aqua, -ae 1 f.	*water*
arma, armorum 2 n. pl.	*arms, weapons*
attonitus, -a, -um	*amazed*
audax, audacis	*bold, daring*
audio, -ire, -ivi 4	*hear, listen to*
aurum, -i 2 n.	*gold*
aut	*or*
autem	*however*
auxilium, -i n.	*help*
bellum gero, -ere, gessi 3	*wage war*
bellum, -i 2 n.	*war*
bene	*well*
bibo, -ere, bibi 3	*drink*
bonus, -a, -um	*good*
cado, -ere, cecidi 3	*fall*
caelum, -i 2 n.	*sky*
canto, -are, -avi, -atum 1	*sing*
capio, -ere, cepi $3\frac{1}{2}$	*take, capture*
carus, -a, -um	*dear*

celeriter	*quickly*
celo, -are, -avi 1	*hide*
cena, -ae 1 f.	*dinner*
cep-	*see* capio
ceteri, -ae, -a	*the rest of*
cibus, -i 2 m.	*food*
circum + accusative	*around*
civis, civis 3 m.	*citizen*
clamo, -are, -avi 1	*shout*
clamor, clamoris 3 m.	*shout*
clarus, -a, -um	*clear, bright, famous*
colligo, -ere, collegi 3	*collect*
comes, comitis 3 m./f.	*companion*
coniunx, coniugis 3 m./f.	*husband, wife*
conspex-	*see* conspicio
conspicio, -ere, conspexi $3^1/_2$	*catch sight of*
constituo, -ere, constitui 3	*decide*
consumo, -ere, consumpsi 3	*eat*
contra + accusative	*against*
convoco, -are, -avi 1	*call together*
copiae, copiarum 1 f. pl.	*troops, forces*
corpus, corporis 3 n.	*body*
cras	*tomorrow*
crudelis, -is, -e	*cruel*
cucurr-	*see* curro
cum + ablative	*with*
cum + subjunctive	*while, since, when*
cupio, -ere, cupivi $3^1/_2$	*want, desire*
cur?	*why?*
curo, -are, -avi 1	*look after, care for*
curro, -ere, cucurri 3	*run*
de + ablative	*down from, about*
dea, -ae 1 f.	*goddess*
debeo, -ere, debui 2	*ought to, must, should*
decem	*ten*
decimus, -a, -um	*tenth*
ded-	*see* do
defendo, -ere, defendi 3	*defend*
deinde	*then, next*
deleo, -ere, delevi 2	*destroy*
deus, dei 2 m.	*god*
dico, -ere, dixi 3	*say*
difficilis, -is, -e	*difficult*
discedo, -ere, discessi 3	*depart*
diu	*for a long time*
dives, divitis	*rich*

divitiae, divitiarum 1 f.pl.	*wealth, riches*
dix-	*see* dico
do, dare, dedi 1	*give*
dominus, -i 2 m.	*master*
domus, -us 4 f.	*home, house*
donum, -i 2 n.	*gift*
dormio, -ire, dormivi 4	*sleep*
duco, -ere, duxi 3	*lead*
duo	*two*
duodecim	*twelve*
duodeviginti	*eighteen*
dux-	*see* duco
dux, ducis 3 m.	*leader, general*
e/ex + ablative	*out of*
effugio, -ere, effugi $3^1/_2$	*escape*
eg-	*see* ago
ego	*I*
egredior, egredi, egressus $3^1/_2$	*go out, leave*
eligo, -ere, elegi 3	*select, choose*
enim (2nd word)	*for*
eo, ire, ii/ivi (irreg.)	*go*
equus, -i 2 m.	*horse*
erro, -are, -avi 1	*be wrong, wander*
esse	*see* sum
et	*and*
et... et...	*both... and...*
etiam	*even, also*
exeo, exire, exii (irreg.)	*go out*
exercitus, -us 4 m.	*army*
exspecto, -are, -avi 1	*wait, wait for*
facilis, -is, -e	*easy*
facio, -ere, feci $3^1/_2$	*do, make*
fec-	*see* facio
felix, felicis	*lucky, fortunate*
femina, -ae 1 f.	*woman*
fessus, -a, -um	*tired*
festino, -are, -avi 1	*hurry*
filia, -ae 1 f.	*daughter*
filius, -i 2 m.	*son*
fio, fieri, factus (irreg.)	*become, am made*
fleo, -ere, flevi 2	*cry*
flev-	*see* fleo
flumen, fluminis 3 n.	*river*
forte	*by chance*
fortis, -is, -e	*brave*

fortiter	*bravely*
frater, fratris 3 m.	*brother*
frustra	*in vain*
fu-	*see* sum
fuga, -ae f.	*escape*
fugio, -ere, fugi $3^1/_2$	*flee*
gladius, -i 2 m.	*sword*
Graecus, -a, -um	*Greek*
habeo, -ere, habui 2	*have*
habito, -are, -avi 1	*live*
hasta, -ae 1 f.	*spear*
heri	*yesterday*
hic	*here*
hic, haec, hoc	*this*
hodie	*today*
homo, hominis 3 m./f.	*man, person*
hostes, hostium 3 m. pl.	*enemy*
i-	*see* eo
iaceo, -ere, iacui 2	*lie (down)*
iacio, -ere, ieci $3^1/_2$	*throw*
iam	*now, already*
ibi	*there*
iec-	*see* iacio
igitur	*therefore*
ille, illa, illud	*that*
in + ablative	*in, on*
in + accusative	*into*
incipio, -ere, incepi $3^1/_2$	*begin*
incola, -ae 1 m./f.	*inhabitant*
ineo, inire, inii (irreg.)	*go in*
ingens, ingentis	*huge*
inquit / inquiunt	*he said, she said / they said*
insula, -ae 1 f.	*island*
inter + accusative	*among, between*
intro, -are, -avi 1	*enter*
invenio, -ire, inveni 4	*find*
ira, -ae 1 f.	*anger*
iratus, -a, -um	*angry*
is, ea, id	*he, she, it; that*
ita	*in such a way*
itaque	*and so*
iter, itineris 3 n.	*journey*
iterum	*again*
itiner-	*see* iter

iubeo, -ere, iussi 2	*order*
iuss-	*see* iubeo
iuvenis, iuvenis 3 m.	*young man*
iv-	*see* eo
laboro, -are, -avi 1	*work*
laetus, -a, -um	*happy*
laudo, -are, -avi 1	*praise*
lectus, -i m.	*bed*
lego, -ere, legi 3	*read, choose*
liber, libri 2 m.	*book*
liberi, -orum 2 m. pl.	*children*
libero, -are, -avi 1	*set free*
limen, liminis 3 n.	*doorway*
litus, litoris 3 n.	*beach, shore*
locus, -i 2 m.	*place*
longus, -a, -um	*long*
luc-	*see* lux
ludo, -ere, lusi 3	*play*
lus-	*see* ludo
lux, lucis 3 f.	*light*
magister, -tri 2 m.	*teacher, master*
magnopere	*greatly*
magnus, -a, -um	*big, great*
maior, maioris	*bigger (comparative of* magnus*)*
malus, -a, -um	*bad, wicked*
maneo, -ere, mansi 2	*stay, remain*
mans-	*see* maneo
manus, -us 4 f.	*hand*
mare, maris 3 n.	*sea*
mater, matris 3 f.	*mother*
maximus, -a, -um	*very big, biggest (superlative of* magnus*)*
medius, -a, -um	*middle of*
melior, melioris	*better (comparative of* bonus*)*
meus, -a, -um	*my*
miles, militis 3 m.	*soldier*
milit-	*see* miles
minimus, -a, -um	*smallest, very small (superlative of* parvus*)*
minor, minoris	*smaller (comparative of* parvus*)*
mis-	*see* mitto
miser, -era, -erum	*wretched*
mitto, -ere, misi 3	*send*
moneo, -ere, monui 2	*warn*
mons, montis 3 m.	*mountain*

mora, -ae 1 f.	*delay*
mors, mortis 3 f.	*death*
mortuus, -a, -um	*dead*
moveo, -ere, movi 2	*move*
mox	*soon*
mulier, mulieris 3 f.	*woman*
multus, -a, -um	*much, many*
murus, -i 2 m.	*wall*
nam	*for*
narro, -are, -avi 1	*tell*
nauta, -ae 1 f.	*sailor*
navigo, -are, -avi 1	*sail*
navis, navis 3 f.	*ship*
-ne?	*(open question)*
neco, -are, -avi 1	*kill*
nemo	*no-one*
nescio, -ire, nescivi 4	*not know*
nihil	*nothing*
nobilis, -is, -e	*noble*
noli, nolite + infinitive	*do not...!*
nomen, nominis 3 n.	*name*
non	*not*
nonne...?	*expects the answer yes*
nonus, -a, -um	*ninth*
nos	*we*
noster, nostra, nostrum	*our*
notus, -a, -um	*well known*
novem	*nine*
novus, -a, -um	*new*
nox, noctis 3 f.	*night*
nullus, -a, -um	*no, none*
num...?	*expects the answer no*
numquam	*never*
nunc	*now*
nuntio, -are, -avi 1	*announce*
nuntius, -i 2 m.	*messenger*
occido, -ere, occidi 3	*kill*
occupo, -are, -avi 1	*seize*
octavus, -a, -um	*eighth*
octo	*eight*
olim	*once (upon a time)*
omnes	*everyone*
omnia	*everything*
omnis, -is, -e	*all, every*
oper-	*see opus*

oppidum, -i 2 n.	*town*
oppugno, -are, -avi 1	*attack*
optimus, -a, -um	*best, very good (superlative of bonus)*
opus, operis 3 n.	*task*
ostendo, -ere, ostendi 3	*show*
parens, parentis 3 m./f.	*parent*
paro, -are, -avi 1	*prepare*
pars, partis 3 f.	*part*
parvus, -a, -um	*small, little*
pater, patris 3 m.	*father*
patria, -ae 1 f.	*country, homeland*
pauci, -ae, -a	*few*
pauper, pauperis	*poor*
pecunia, -ae 1 f.	*money*
per + accusative	*through, along*
peior, peioris	*worse (comparative of malus)*
pereo, perire, perii (irreg.)	*perish*
periculum, -i 2 n.	*danger*
perterritus, -a, -um	*frightened*
pessimus, -a, -um	*worst, very bad (superlative of malus)*
plurimus, -a, -um	*very many, most (superlative of multus)*
plus, pluris	*more (comparative of multus)*
poeta, -ae 1 m.	*poet*
pono, -ere, posui 3	*put*
porto, -are, -avi 1	*carry*
portus, -us 4 m.	*harbour*
posit-	*see pono*
possum, posse, potui (irreg.)	*be able, can*
post + accusative	*after*
postea	*later*
postquam	*after*
posu-	*see pono*
potu-	*see possum*
primus, -a, -um	*first*
pro + ablative	*for*
proelium, -i 2 n.	*battle*
prope + accusative	*near*
propter + accusative	*on account of, because of*
puella, -ae 1 f.	*girl*
puer, pueri 2 m.	*boy*
pugno, -are, -avi 1	*fight*
pulcher, pulchra, pulchrum	*beautiful, handsome*
punio, -ire, -ivi 4	*punish*
puto, -are, -avi 1	*think*
quam	*than*

quamquam	*although*
quartus, -a, -um	*fourth*
quattuor	*four*
quattuordecim	*fourteen*
-que	*and*
quid?	*what?*
quindecim	*fifteen*
quinque	*five*
quintus, -a, -um	*fifth*
quis?	*who?*
quo	*where…to*
quod	*because*
quoque	*also*
rect-	*see* rego
redeo, redire, redii (irreg.)	*go back, return*
reduco, -ere, reduxi 3	*lead back*
regia, -ae 1 f.	*palace*
regina, -ae 1 f.	*queen*
rego, -ere, rexi 3	*rule*
relinquo, -ere, reliqui 3	*abandon, leave behind*
respondeo, -ere, respondi 2	*answer*
rex-	*see* rego
rex, regis 3 m.	*king*
rideo, -ere, risi 2	*laugh*
ris-	*see* rideo
rogo, -are, -avi 1	*ask, ask for*
Romanus, -a, -um	*Roman*
ruo, -ere, rui 3	*charge*
sacer, sacra, sacrum	*sacred*
saepe	*often*
saevus, -a, -um	*savage*
sagitta, -ae 1 f.	*arrow*
saluto, -are, -avi 1	*greet*
sapiens, sapientis	*wise*
scribo, -ere, scripsi 3	*write*
scrips-	*see* scribo
scutum, -i 2 n.	*shield*
se	*himself, herself, themselves*
secundus, -a, -um	*second*
sed	*but*
sedecim	*sixteen*
sedeo, -ere, sedi 2	*sit*
semper	*always*
senex, senis 3 m.	*old man*
septem	*seven*

septimus, -a, -um	*seventh*
servo, -are, -avi 1	*save*
servus, -i 2 m.	*slave*
sex	*six*
sextus, -a, -um	*sixth*
sic	*thus*
silentium, -i 2 n.	*silence*
sine + ablative	*without*
socius, -i 2 m.	*ally*
sollicitus, -a, -um	*worried*
solus, -a, -um	*alone*
soror, sororis 3 f.	*sister*
specto, -are, -avi 1	*watch, look at*
statim	*immediately*
stet-	*see* sto
sto, -are, steti 1	*stand*
sub + ablative	*under*
subito	*suddenly*
sum, esse, fui (irreg.)	*be*
super + accusative	*above*
supero, -are, -avi 1	*overcome*
surgo, -ere, surrexi 3	*get up*
suus, -a, -um	*his own, her own, their own*
talis, -is, -e	*such, of such a kind*
tamen	*however*
tandem	*at last*
telum, -i 2 n.	*spear, javelin*
templum, -i 2 n.	*temple*
teneo, -ere, tenui 2	*hold*
terra, -ae 1 f.	*land*
terreo, -ere, terrui 2	*frighten*
tertius, -a, -um	*third*
timeo, -ere 2	*fear, am afraid*
trado, -ere, tradidi 3	*hand over*
trans + accusative	*across*
transeo, transire, transii (irreg.)	*go across, cross*
tredecim	*thirteen*
tres	*three*
tristis, -is, -e	*sad*
tu	*you* (singular)
tul-	*see* fero
tum	*then*
tumultus, -us 4 m.	*uproar*
turba, -ae 1 f.	*crowd*
tutus, -a, -um	*safe*
tuus, -a, -um	*your* (singular)

ubi	*when*
ubi?	*where?*
una	*together*
unda, -ae 1 f.	*wave*
unde	*where… from*
undecim	*eleven*
undeviginti	*nineteen*
unus	*one*
urbs, urbis 3 f.	*city*
ut + indicative	*when, as*
uxor, uxoris 3 f.	*wife*
validus, -a, -um	*strong*
venio, -ire, veni 4	*come*
ventus, -i 2 m.	*wind*
verbum, -i 2 n.	*word*
vester, vestra, vestrum	*your* (plural)
vetus, veteris	*old*
via, -ae 1 f.	*road, street*
vic-	*see* vinco
video, -ere, vidi 2	*see*
viginti	*twenty*
villa, -ae 1 f.	*villa*
vinco, -ere, vici 3	*conquer, beat, defeat, win*
vinum, -i 2 n.	*wine*
vir, viri 2 m.	*man*
virtus, virtutis 3 f.	*courage*
vivus, -a, -um	*alive*
voco, -are, -avi 1	*call*
vos	*you* (plural)
vox, vocis 3 f.	*voice*
vulnero, -are, -avi 1	*wound*
vulnus, vulneris 3 n.	*wound*

Vocabulary: English-Latin

(open question)	-ne?
abandon	relinquo, -ere, reliqui 3
able, be	possum, posse, potui (irreg.)
about	de + ablative
above	super + accusative
across	trans + accusative
after (preposition)	post + accusative
after (conjunction)	postquam
again	iterum
against	contra + accusative
alive	vivus, -a, -um
all	omnis, -is, -e
ally	socius, -i 2 m.
alone	solus, -a, -um
along	per + accusative
already	iam
also	quoque; etiam
although	quamquam
always	semper
amazed	attonitus, -a, -um
among	inter + accusative
and	et; -que
and so	itaque
anger	ira, -ae 1 f.
angry	iratus, -a, -um
announce	nuntio, -are, -avi 1
answer	respondeo, -ere, respondi 2
approach	appropinquo, -are, -avi, 1
arms	arma, armorum 2 n. pl.
army	exercitus, -us 4 m.
around	circum + accusative
arrive	advenio, -ire, adveni 4
arrow	sagitta, -ae 1 f.
as	ut + indicative
ask, ask for	rogo, -are, -avi 1
at last	tandem
attack	oppugno, -are, -avi 1
bad	malus, -a, -um
battle	proelium, -i 2 n.
be	sum, esse, fui irreg.
be able	possum, posse, potui (irreg.)
be afraid of	timeo, -ere 2
be away, be absent	absum, abesse, afui (irreg.)

be present	adsum, adesse, adfui (irreg.)
be wrong	erro, -are, -avi 1
beach	litus, litoris 3 n.
beat	vinco, -ere, vici 3
beautiful	pulcher, pulchra, pulchrum
because	quod
because of	propter + accusative
bed	lectus, -i 2 m.
before (conjunction)	antequam
before (preposition)	ante + accusative
begin	incipio, --ere, incepi $3\frac{1}{2}$
believe	credo, -ere, credidi + dative 3
between	inter + accusative
big	magnus, -a, -um
body	corpus, corporis 3 n.
bold	audax, audacis
book	liber, libri 2 m.
both... and...	et... et...
boy	puer, pueri 2 m.
brave	fortis, -is, -e
bravely	fortiter
bright	clarus, -a, -um
brother	frater, fratris 3 m.
build	aedifico, -are, -avi 1
but	sed
by	a/ab + ablative
by chance	forte
call	voco, -are, -avi 1
call together	convoco, -are, -avi 1
can	possum, posse, potui (irreg.)
capture	capio, -ere, cepi $3\frac{1}{2}$
care for	curo, -are, -avi 1
carry	porto, -are, -avi 1;
catch sight of	conspicio, -ere, conspexi $3\frac{1}{2}$
charge	ruo, -ere, rui 3
children	liberi, -orum 2 m. pl.
choose	lego, -ere, legi, lectum 3;
	eligo, -ere, elegi, electum 3
citizen	civis, civis 3 m.
city	urbs, urbis 3 f.
clear	clarus, -a, -um
collect	colligo, -ere, collegi 3
come	venio, -ire, veni 4
companion	comes, comitis 3 m./f.
conquer	vinco, -ere, vici 3
country	patria, -ae 1 f.

courage	virtus, virtutis 3 f.
cross	transeo, transire, transii (irreg.)
crowd	turba, -ae 1 f.
cruel	crudelis, -is, -e
cry	fleo, -ere, flevi 2
danger	periculum, -i 2 n.
daring	audax, audacis
daughter	filia, -ae 1 f.
dead	mortuus, -a, -um
dear	carus, -a, -um
death	mors, mortis 3 f.
decide	constituo, -ere, constitui 3
deep	altus, -a, -um
defeat	vinco, -ere, vici 3
defend	defendo, -ere, defendi 3
delay	mora, -ae 1 f.
depart	discedo, -ere, discessi 3
desire	cupio, -ere, cupivi $3\frac{1}{2}$
destroy	deleo, -ere, delevi 2
difficult	difficilis, -is, -e
dinner	cena, -ae 1 f.
do	facio, -ere, feci $3\frac{1}{2}$;
	ago, -ere, egi 3
do not...!	noli, nolite + infinitive
doorway	limen, liminis 3 n.
down from	de + ablative
drink	bibo, -ere, bibi 3
drive	pello, -ere, pepuli, pulsum 3
drop	cado, -ere, cecidi 3
easy	facilis, -is, -e
eat	consumo, -ere, consumpsi 3
eight	octo
eighteen	duodeviginti
eighth	octavus, -a, -um
eleven	undecim
enemy	hostes, hostium 3 m. pl.
enter	intro, -are, -avi 1
escape (noun)	fuga, -ae 1 f.
escape (verb)	effugio, -ere, effugi $3\frac{1}{2}$
even	etiam
every	omnis, -is -e
everyone	omnes
everything	omnia
expects the answer *no*	num...?
expects the answer *yes*	nonne...?

fall	cado, -ere, cecidi 3
famous	clarus, -a, -um
farmer	agricola, -ae 1 m.
father	pater, patris 3 m.
fear	timeo, -ere, timui 2;
few	pauci, -ae, -a
field	ager, agri 2 m.
fifteen	quindecim
fifth	quintus, -a, -um
fight	pugno, -are, -avi 1
find	invenio, -ire, inveni 4
first	primus, -a, -um
five	quinque
flee	fugio, -ere, fugi $3\frac{1}{2}$
food	cibus, -i 2 m.
for	nam; pro + ablative; enim
for a long time	diu
forces	copiae, copiarum 1 f. pl.
fortunate	felix, felicis
four	quattuor
fourteen	quattuordecim
fourth	quartus, -a, -um
friend	amicus, -i 2 m.
frighten	terreo, -ere, terrui 2
frightened	perterritus, -a, -um
from	a/ab + ablative
front of, in	ante + accusative
general	dux, ducis 3 m.
get up	surgo, -ere, surrexi 3
gift	donum, -i 2 n.
girl	puella, -ae 1 f.
give	do, -dare, dedi 1
go	eo, ire, ii/ivi (irreg.)
go across	transeo, transire, transii (irreg.)
go back	redeo, redire, redii (irreg.)
go in	ineo, inire, inii (irreg.)
go out	exeo, exire, exii (irreg
go towards	adeo, adire, adii (irreg.)
god	deus, dei 2 m.
goddess	dea, -ae 1 f.
gold	aurum, -i 2 n.
good	bonus, -a, -um
great	magnus, -a -um
greatly	magnopere
Greek	Graecus, -a, -um

greet	saluto, -are, -avi 1
hand	manus, -us 4 f.
hand over	trado, -ere, tradidi 3
handsome	pulcher, pulchra, pulchrum
happy	laetus, -a, -um
harbour	portus, -us 4 m.
have	habeo, -ere, habui 2
he said	inquit
he, she, it	is, ea, id
hear	audio, -ire, -ivi 4
help (noun)	auxilium, -i n.
her (own)	suus, -a, -um
here	hic
herself	se
hide	celo, -are, -avi 1
high	altus, -a, -um
him	(is the accusative of *he*)
himself	se
his (own)	suus, -a, -um
hold	teneo, -ere, tenui 2
home	domus, -us 4 f.
homeland	patria, -ae 1 f.
horse	equus, -i 2 m.
house	domus, -us 4 f.
however	autem; tamen
huge	ingens, ingentis
hurry	festino, -are, -avi 1
husband	coniunx, coniugis 3 m.
I	ego
immediately	statim
in	in + ablative
in vain	frustra
inhabitant	incola, -ae 1 m./f.
into	in + accusative
island	insula, -ae 1 f.
javelin	telum, -i 2 n.
journey	iter, itineris 3 n.
kill	neco, -are, -avi 1; occido, -ere, occidi 3
king	rex, regis 3 m.
land	terra, -ae 1 f.
later	postea

laugh	rideo, -ere, risi 2
lead	duco, -ere, duxi 3
lead back	reduco, -ere, reduxi 3
leader	dux, ducis 3 m.
leave (= depart)	discedo, -ere, discessi 3
leave behind	relinquo, -ere, reliqui 3
lie (down)	iaceo, -ere, iacui 2
light	lux, lucis 3 f.
like	amo, -are, -avi 1
listen to	audio, -ire, -ivi 4
little	parvus, -a, -um
live	habito, -are, -avi 1
long	longus, -a, -um
look after	curo, -are, -avi 1
look at	specto, -are, -avi 1
love	amo, -are, -avi 1
lucky	felix, felicis
maidservant	ancilla, -ae 1 f.
make	facio, -ere, feci, factum $3\frac{1}{2}$
man	vir, viri 2 m.; homo, hominis 3 m./f.
many	multi, multae, multa (plural)
master	dominus, -i 2 m.
master (teacher)	magister, -tri 2 m.
meanwhile	interea
messenger	nuntius, -i 2 m.
middle of	medius, -a, -um
money	pecunia, -ae 1 f.
mother	mater, matris 3 f.
mountain	mons, montis 3 m.
move	moveo, -ere, movi, motum 2
much	multus, -a, -um
must	debeo, -ere, debui, debitum 2
my	meus, -a, -um
myself	me
name	nomen, nominis 3 n.
near	prope + accusative
never	numquam
new	novus, -a, -um
nine	novem
nineteen	undeviginti
ninth	nonus, -a, -um
no	nullus, -a, -um
noble	nobilis, -is, -e
none	nullus, -a, -um
no-one	nemo

not	non
nothing	nihil
not want	nolo, nolle, nolui (irreg.)
now	iam; nunc
often	saepe
old	vetus, veteris
old man	senex, senis 3 m.
on	in + ablative
on account of	propter + accusative
once (upon a time)	olim
one	unus
or	aut
order	iubeo, -ere, iussi 2
other	alius
ought	debeo, -ere, debui 2
our	noster, nostra, nostrum
out of	e/ex + ablative
overcome	supero, -are, -avi 1
palace	regia, -ae 1 f.
parent	parens, parentis 3 m./f.
part	pars, partis 3 f.
perish	pereo, perire, perii (irreg.)
person	homo, hominis 3 m./f.
place	locus, -i 2 m.
play	ludo, -ere, lusi 3
poet	poeta, -ae 1 m.
poor	pauper, pauperis
praise	laudo, -are, -avi 1
prepare	paro, -are, -avi 1
punish	punio, -ire, -ivi 4
put	pono, -ere, posui 3
queen	regina, -ae 1 f.
quickly	celeriter
race	gens, gentis 3 f.
read	lego, -ere, legi 3
receive	accipio, -ere, accepi $3\frac{1}{2}$
remain	maneo, -ere, mansi 2
rest of, the	ceteri, -ae, -a
return	redeo, redire, redii (irreg.)
rich	dives, divitis
riches	divitiae, divitiarum 1 f. pl.
river	flumen, fluminis 3 n.
road	via, -ae 1 f.

Roman	Romanus, -a, -um
rule	rego, -ere, rexi 3
run	curro, -ere, cucurri 3
sacred	sacer, sacra, sacrum
sad	tristis, -is, -e
safe	tutus, -a, -um
sail	navigo, -are, -avi 1
sailor	nauta, -ae 1 f.
savage	saevus, -a, -um
save	servo, -are, -avi 1
say	dico, -ere, dixi 3
sea	mare, maris 3 n.
second	secundus, -a, -um
see	video, -ere, vidi 2
seize	occupo, -are, -avi 1
select	eligo, -ere, elegi 3
send	mitto, -ere, misi 3
set free	libero, -are, -avi 1
seven	septem
seventeen	septendecim
seventh	septimus, -a, -um
she said	inquit
shield	scutum, -i 2 n.
ship	navis, navis 3 f.
shore	litus, litoris 3 n.
should	debeo, -ere, debui 2
shout (noun)	clamor, clamoris 3 m.
shout (verb)	clamo, -are, -avi 1
show	ostendo, -ere, ostendi 3
silence	silentium, -i 2 n.
sing	canto, -are, -avi 1
sister	soror, sororis 3 f.
sit	sedeo, -ere, sedi 2
six	sex
sixth	sextus, -a, -um
sky	caelum, -i 2 n.
slave	servus, -i 2 m.
sleep (verb)	dormio, -ire, dormivi 4
slowly	lente
small	parvus, -a, -um
soldier	miles, militis 3 m.
son	filius, -i 2 m.
soon	mox
spear	hasta, -ae 1 f.; telum, -i 2 n.
stand	sto, -are, steti 1
stay	maneo, -ere, mansi 2

street	via, -ae 1 f.
strong	validus, -a, -um
suddenly	subito
sword	gladius, -i 2 m.
take	capio, -ere, cepi $3\frac{1}{2}$
task	opus, operis 3 n.
teacher	magister, -tri 2 m.
tell	narro, -are, -avi 1
temple	templum, -i 2 n.
ten	decem
tenth	decimus, -a, -um
than	quam
that	ille, illa, illud
the rest of	ceteri, -ae, -a
their (own)	suus, -a, -um
themselves	se
then	tum
then, next	deinde
there	ibi
therefore	igitur
these	(is the plural of *this*)
think	puto, -are, -avi 1
third	tertius, -a, -um
thirteen	tredecim
this	hic, haec, hoc
those	(is the plural of *that*)
three	tres
through	per + accusative
throw	iacio, -ere, ieci $3\frac{1}{2}$
thus	sic
tired	fessus, -a, -um
to (= towards)	ad + accusative
today	hodie
together	una
tomorrow	cras
towards	ad + accusative
town	oppidum, -i 2 n.
troops	copiae, copiarum 1 f. pl.
twelve	duodecim
twenty	viginti
two	duo
under	sub + ablative
uproar	tumultus, -us 4 m.
vain, in	frustra

villa	villa, -ae 1 f.
voice	vox, vocis 3 f.
wage war	bellum gero, -ere, gessi 3
wait, wait for	exspecto, -are, -avi 1
walk	ambulo, -are, -avi 1
wall	murus, -i 2 m.
wander	erro, -are, -avi 1
want	cupio, -ere, cupivi, cupitum $3\frac{1}{2}$
war	bellum, -i 2 n.
warn	moneo, -ere, monui 2
watch	specto, -are, -avi 1
water	aqua, -ae 1 f.
wave	unda, -ae 1 f.
we	nos
wealth	divitiae, divitiarum 1 f. pl.
weapons	arma, armorum 2 n. pl.
well	bene
well known	notus, -a, -um
what?	quid?
when	ubi; ut + indicative
where?	ubi?
where,,, from	unde
where… to	quo
who?	quis?
why?	cur?
wicked	malus, -a, -um
wife	uxor, uxoris 3 f.; coniunx, coniugis 3 m./f.
win	vinco, -ere, vici, victum 3
wind	ventus, -i 2 m.
wine	vinum, -i 2 n.
wise	sapiens, sapientis
wish	cupio, -ere, cupivi $3\frac{1}{2}$
with	cum + ablative
within	(use an ablative of time expression)
without	sine + ablative
woman	femina, -ae 1 f.; mulier, mulieris 3 f.
word	verbum, -i 2 n.
work (noun)	labor, laboris 3 m.
work (verb)	laboro, -are, -avi 1
worried	sollicitus, -a, -um
wound (noun)	vulnus, vulneris n.
wound (verb)	vulnero, -are, -avi 1
wretched	miser, -era, -erum
write	scribo, -ere, scripsi 3
wrong, be	erro, -are, -avi 1

yesterday	heri
you (plural)	vos
you (singular)	tu
young man	iuvenis, iuvenis 3 m.
your (plural)	vester, vestra, vestrum
your (singular)	tuus, -a, -um
yourself	te
yourselves	vos

Printed in Great Britain
by Amazon